Bulletin 64
1954

THE SOCIAL SCIENCES
IN HISTORICAL STUDY

A Report of the
Committee on Historiography

SOCIAL SCIENCE RESEARCH COUNCIL
230 PARK AVENUE   NEW YORK 17

907
S678s

45147

The Social Science Research Council was organized in 1923 and formally incorporated in 1924 for the purpose of advancing research in the social sciences. Its members are chosen from seven associated professional organizations in the social sciences and from related fields.

ASSOCIATED ORGANIZATIONS

American Anthropological Association

American Economic Association

American Historical Association

American Political Science Association

American Psychological Association

American Sociological Society

American Statistical Association

COMMITTEE ON HISTORIOGRAPHY

FOREWORD

As explained at greater length in the introductory chapter, the present volume had its origin in the reception accorded the published report of the Council's earlier Committee on Historiography, 1943–45. The stimulating discussion of that report, *Theory and Practice in Historical Study,* Social Science Research Council Bulletin 54, in critical reviews; the initiative of Jeannette P. Nichols in arranging for intensive consideration of the Bulletin's contributions and implications for future historical research, at a session of the 1947 annual meeting of the American Historical Association; the comparable programs at meetings of that Association's Pacific Coast Branch and of the Mississippi Valley Historical Association in 1948—all these confirmed the judgment of the Council that the interest of historians in extending and improving their methods and approaches deserved further encouragement and support.

It is gratifying to present this report of the Council's second Committee on Historiography, prepared wholly through the voluntary efforts of its individual members, past and present. In the words of Dr. Nichols, concluding her introductory chapter, the Council like the Committee makes "no claim to significant originality, far less to finality," in the conclusions presented. The report is offered for consideration by historians "in the hope that, like its predecessor, it will stimulate serious thought, fruitful discussion, and constructive criticism."

PENDLETON HERRING

ACKNOWLEDGMENTS

This report is a product of group thinking. Much of the orientation and basic theory stems from contributions by Committee members who were absent in the final stage of preparation: notably, Ralph E. Turner, the first chairman, who led discussions with outside experts and presented interim papers on demography and anthropology; and Eugene N. Anderson, who participated actively in early discussions. The ascription of authorship for particular chapters is justifiable only in the sense that initial drafts were the work of those designated. The final draft reflected the pooled judgments of all concerned. Individual credit should nevertheless be given. Chapter 1 was contributed by Jeannette P. Nichols; Chapter 2 was the joint product of Hugh G. J. Aitken and Bert James Loewenberg; Chapters 3 and 7 were assigned to Thomas C. Cochran; Chapters 4 and 6 were contributed by Samuel Hugh Brockunier, assisted in the final revision by Bert James Loewenberg; Chapter 5 was the assignment of Shepard B. Clough. Ralph E. Turner's labors as editor of the UNESCO world history series compelled release from his original assignment of Chapters 2 and 4, but the Committee had the benefit of his critical comment on the first draft of the manuscript. All members of the Committee contributed materials and suggestions for chapters other than their own. To its indefatigable editor, Hugh G. J. Aitken, the Committee owes a special debt for searching criticism and important revisions. Warm acknowledgment is due to the distinguished social scientists who served as consultants: for anthropology, to A. L. Kroeber and Clyde Kluckhohn; for demography, to Joseph J. Spengler; for economics, to A. G. Hart; for psychology, to Gardner Murphy and Eugene L. Hartley; for political science, to E. E. Schattschneider; for sociology, to Harry Alpert. Valuable suggestions at the final stage of revision were received from various outside experts: Leonard S. Cottrell, Jr., David Easton, Oliver Garceau, A. Irving Hallowell, Pendleton Herring, E. P. Hutchinson, V. O. Key, M. Brewster Smith, and Donald Young.

CONTENTS

1 INTRODUCTION: THE BACKGROUND OF BULLETIN 64

ROBERT BURNS was echoing a familiar plaint when in 1786 he indited his ode "To a Louse" with these remorseful words:

> O wad some Pow'r the giftie gie us,
> To see oursels as ithers see us!
> It wad frae mony a blunder free us
> An' foolish notion:
> What airs in dress an' gait wad lea'e us,
> An' ev'n devotion!

Not too self-confident, now and then, to peer earnestly through the microscope of self-analysis, some historians can on occasion frankly acknowledge a craving for self-improvement. Such a craving ten years ago led the Social Science Research Council to sponsor the attempt of a group of cooperating scholars to re-examine the functions and methods of history—an attempt that resulted in the publication in 1946 of Council Bulletin 54, *Theory and Practice in Historical Study: A Report of the Committee on Historiography*. The persistence of that craving has led in turn to this second bulletin under the same sponsorship. Ever since 1910 minorities in the American Historical Association have been stirring up controversies stimulating to thought about historical methods and interpretation; this bulletin may therefore be said to be continuing a tradition nearly half a century old.

As the peculiar identification of historians is their preoccupation with events moving in time, it may be useful to introduce the 1954 bulletin with mention of three aspects of its background: a brief reminder of the nature of its predecessor; a brief summary of some significant reactions of scholars to that effort; and mention of shifting emphases in American historiography since 1946.

THE SCOPE OF BULLETIN 54

Motivated to provide "a manual designed to help clarify thought about history and to aid historians in teaching and writing it," [1] the earlier Committee after much labor and serious disappointments pro-

---

[1] Merle Curti, "Foreword," Bulletin 54, p. vii.

duced a 177-page report by six authors, whose work was strained through the sieve of Committee reactions before appearing in final form. The report contains the following chapters:

I. "Grounds for a Reconsideration of Historiography" by Charles A. Beard;

II. "Controlling Assumptions in the Practice of American Historians" by John Herman Randall, Jr. and George Haines, IV;

III. "What Historians Have Said about the Causes of the Civil War" by Howard K. Beale;

IV. "Problems of Terminology in Historical Writing," containing a note on the need for greater precision, by Beard, and detailed discussion of illustrative terms by Sidney Hook;

V. "Propositions," embodying Committee thought on 21 basic premises;

VI. "Selective Reading List on Historiography and the Philosophy of History" compiled by Ronald Thompson.

Anyone reading these chapters carefully must agree that the report "is not and does not aim to be a systematic, comprehensive treatise on historical method. It is, rather, a collection of related essays, by several accomplished contributors, on aspects of historiography." [2] Such a reader must also note that the report "makes no claim to having 'settled' any of the issues with which it has dealt." [3] Yet it has unity. Its unity derives from the fact that the Committee was animated by a mutually held conviction—the conviction that historians should try to interpret or understand history so as to make written history "at least a cumulative body of knowledge useful as a guide in solving our present problems of human relations." [4]

Concerning the probable reception of their report, the Committee of course did not expect either universal interest or eager acclaim. They knew better. They knew that only the rash classify historians into general categories, even such loose ones as "conservatives" or "liberals," since historians actually are highly individualistic. Reminders of this had come repeatedly during the labors of the Committee, from among the members themselves and from others. For example, a Committee request for criticism of a projected set of propositions was ignored by

---

[2] Fulmer Mood, *Pacific Historical Review*, 15:438 (December 1946).
[3] Curti, *op. cit.*, p. ix.
[4] Crane Brinton, *Journal of Modern History*, 18:342 (December 1946).

50 percent of the 70 historians to whom it was addressed. The remainder reacted, of course, individually, and only the most generalized classification of their opinions was possible. Eight "could in no sense fairly be said to be in even partial agreement"; "twelve were willing to accept several of the propositions, subject to modifications in style." Fifteen, that is approximately one fifth of those queried, "did not seem to be opposed in any fundamental ways to the thought in the Propositions, although many took exception to the style and diction." [5]

Furthermore, when the Committee planned to include in the report definitions of historical terms in the "light" of current usage, they found darkness; usage was uniform only in its lack of uniformity. Consequently, definition of terms was essayed on the individual judgments of a historian and a philosopher.

Moreover, this brain child was entering an unsettled world, wracked by hostilities. Even in less turbulent days some professors have found their students, like themselves, rather annoyed if not actually resentful to learn that there are conflicting interpretations of a development. By the middle 1940's the world emphasis was increasingly shifting toward a "search for security," for "certainty," while Bulletin 54 boldly stressed the pervasiveness of change and of uncertainty. Further, the problems most stressed in that report concerned handicaps suffered by historians through their individual situations and assumptions, problems "relative" to their environment.

"A considerable number of historians will not find this a dish to their liking," remarked an early reviewer.[6] "Yet even though they say that it is spinach and to hell with it, one may also conjecture that there is a good deal in the *Report* that needs to be stomached." This digestive process has no small significance for diagnosticians of the health of the historical body. One becomes curious: how many tried to partake of the dish; how did they react to it?

How many sampled the dish can be estimated only imprecisely. More than 5,600 copies of the volume had been sold up to February 1, 1954, with sales still continuing at the rate of about 30 copies monthly seven years after publication. Some 380 copies had been distributed gratis for review and other purposes. Duplicate copies ordered for the shelves of university libraries indicate that successive groups of seminar students have dipped into the dish.

Most of the reactions to such sampling are not recorded. But records

[5] Curti, *op. cit.*, pp. viii–ix.
[6] Edward W. Strong, *American Historical Review*, 52:98 (October 1946).

are extant for at least three sessions at annual meetings of historians; [7] reviews of Bulletin 54 were written for at least 28 journals; and it inspired several thoughtful articles and sharp controversies in learned periodicals. These addresses, reviews, and articles in themselves have no little significance for the student of American historiography, both despite and because of their diversity. Therefore it seems worth while to attempt to summarize, in part, what is freely admitted to be unsummarizable as a whole. At least it may be ventured that quasi uniformity emerges in one respect: Each commentator seemed to be led by his "frame of reference" [8] to write much the sort of review that friends familiar with his life experience would have expected him to write. Let the "relativists" take from that their crumb of comfort.

REACTIONS TO BULLETIN 54

Summary of comment on three of the six chapters is relatively easy because they were almost uniformly praised: Ronald Thompson's "Selective Reading List on Historiography and the Philosophy of History"; Howard Beale's "What Historians Have Said about the Causes of the Civil War"; and Charles A. Beard's "Grounds for a Reconsideration of Historiography." In these chapters most historians found little to discomfort them, encountering familiar things—a bibliographical tool, the long-fought conflict over the causes of the Civil War, and Beardian questioning.

Respecting Thompson's bibliography, a few historians objected because it was deliberately "select" rather than less ambitiously encyclopedic; but mostly it was found useful, good, excellent, in itself making the report worth while. Indeed, to one of the report's severest critics it was "very valuable." [9] Perhaps the most penetrating comment on the bibliography (and on Beard's "Grounds for a Reconsideration") was made by a historian who, referring to their content and range, observed that they represented especially well "the confusions in which most historical students have been tossing." [10]

[7] American Historical Association, Cleveland, December 28, 1947; Mississippi Valley Historical Association, Rock Island, Ill., April 23, 1948; Pacific Coast Branch, American Historical Association, Berkeley, Calif., January 3, 1948.

[8] The frame of reference of the writer is that of one who was, throughout, a member of the Committee that produced Bulletin 54, but who did not become a member of the Committee producing Bulletin 64 until November 1952.

[9] W. Stull Holt, *Pennsylvania Magazine of History*, 72:82 (January 1948).

[10] Frederic C. Lane, *Journal of Economic History*, 7:83 (May 1947).

As a superb demonstration of the prevalence of "confused tossing" in connection with the problem of cause, Beale's analysis of "What Historians Have Said about the Causes of the Civil War" was generally appreciated. The encomium admirable was bestowed on this chapter repeatedly, joined by extremely useful, splendid, judicious, able. Its specific nature brought expressions of relief: "Perhaps because it gets down to brass tacks, it is the most readable and most enjoyable portion of the book." [11]

But it could not go unnoticed that this analysis dealt with "perspectives and loyalties" as applied to cause. Herein both believers and skeptics on relativist implications found reassurance. On the one hand Beale reported that "Heralded 'objectivity' has too often turned out to be mere unawareness of individual prejudice or else an unwitting reflection of the prevailing prejudice of the period or region." But also he voiced belief "that the repeated efforts to discover the 'truth' about causes of the Civil War have been fruitful and that both the methods and the quality of history have improved in the period analyzed." [12] The latter expression of faith was reassurance of progress to historians intent on "objectivity." Conclusions of the former type were cited by historians more addicted to historical theory, as bearing out the report's main thesis that "historical practice cannot do without theory and that overt, critical cognizance of theory is better for practice than unconscious or unacknowledged assumption, selection, and interpretation." [13]

"Grounds for a Reconsideration of Historiography" failed to match Beard's usual achievements in rousing heated controversy. In so far as it was a statement of the importance of studying and writing history, many of the guild found it satisfying, sagacious, excellent, or indeed so lacking in novelty that to one reviewer its omission would have been slight loss. Actually the chapter was intended to focus attention on the basic dilemmas and to challenge historians to thought and action on those dilemmas.

To this end Beard reminded historians that men of affairs ignore the guild and yet continually employ, for their own purposes, assertions as to "what history shows." He asked why, if "history-as-actuality"

[11] Hubert G. Schmidt, *Journal of the Illinois State Historical Society*, 39:380 (September 1946).
[12] Bulletin 54, pp. 91, 90.
[13] Strong, *op. cit.*, p. 99.

(meaning total human experience) permits formulation of hypotheses useful in practical affairs, the western world nevertheless now is confronted by its "most widespread and tumultuous crisis" in thought, learning, and practice, "since the beginning of recorded history." [14] He summoned historians to try to apply themselves to solving a difficult problem: "How can a consensus of competence be secured on the formulas of procedure in historical study and writing best calculated to attain the ends of greater comprehensiveness, exactitude, and utility for theory and practice in the world of thought and action?" [15] This inquiry to one reviewer appeared "perhaps the most challenging sentence in the book"; and to him the eleven pages in this chapter constituted "the most significant speculative part of the volume." [16]

Summary of comment on the three other chapters is relatively difficult because they delved more deeply into theory. There the lack of accepted precision in terminology handicapped both writers and readers. Various commentators interpreted variously, and the "frame of reference" had to be struggled with.

In "Controlling Assumptions in the Practice of American Historians," Randall and Haines attempted a frank comparison of what leading historians have said about the nature and purpose of history and their actual practice of their craft. Naturally, this chapter stimulated more controversy. Appreciative commentators found it in whole or in large part clear, sound, interesting, valuable, thoughtful, penetrating, excellent, brilliant, "an ideal bit of reading" for graduate students,[17] "perhaps the most valuable section," [18] an essay "which should gain acceptance from all but the most devout believers in history *wie es eigentlich gewesen.*" [19]

Others read with a difference. Skeptics on relativism thought the chapter went too far. If a historian deliberately ascertained his "principle of selection" would he not prove more biased than if he simply tried to write "in as detached a manner as possible"? [20] Some felt that the presentation of the views of "scientific" historians like G. B. Adams, Osgood, and Andrews was oversimplified, unfair, and inaccurate; references to Andrews were termed too harsh; Turner appeared over-

14 Bulletin 54, p. 5.
15 *Ibid.,* p. 13.
16 Bert James Loewenberg, *New York History,* 27:506, 505 (October 1946).
17 Lane, *op. cit.,* p. 84.
18 Thomas P. Neill, *Historical Bulletin,* 25:24 (November 1946).
19 Brinton, *op. cit.,* p. 341.
20 John D. Barnhart, *Indiana Magazine of History,* 42:416 (December 1946).

emphasized. A severe critic, dubious concerning the relevance to a manual of historiography of the "connection between the intellectual interests of historians and the social milieu," thought he found here "shallow discussion" and "flimsy generalizations" which to his thinking failed to throw much light upon the nature of history or to lend conviction to the general thesis.[21] "Serious challenges" would arise over the assertion that American historiography came "of age" with recognition of the functional nature of historical knowledge.[22] Another, commenting on this criterion of adulthood, differed as to the time of its possible application; instead of assigning it to the twentieth century, should it not have been moved back to the era of Bancroft?

Some serious students of "objective relativism," on the other hand, did not think that the chapter went far enough and they would have preferred a more comprehensive treatment. One of these said of Bulletin 54 as a whole, "this searching appraisal of historical theory and practice is a vitally important document"; but concerning the chapter by Randall and Haines, "The admirable summary of the functional view of knowledge never comes to grips with the philosophy upon which it is based or the philosophy which opposes it." [23] He considered Randall and Haines "far too optimistic" in concluding that recent historians "have realized more clearly just what it is they are doing." [24] Also, their essay fell between two stools—it was too elliptical for the general reader and too general for the learned.

The plea that historians develop and test hypothetical tools brought the ringing of alarms in other quarters, too. A continuing clash of opposing doctrines was indeed ensured by admitting values to hypothetical status. The authors might well "have indicated more vigorously than they have the dangers as well as the advantages of the use of hypotheses. These have led to much bad history as well as to much good." [25]

Would not prostitution of history, like that by the Nazis, Fascists and Communists, follow from the careless use of values? What if American historians' values were those of the New Deal? Or of "private enterprise"? Debate on this line was revived anew in 1950 when a presidential address before the American Historical Association ex-

---

[21] Oscar Handlin, *New England Quarterly*, 19:538–539 (December 1946).

[22] Herman Ausubel, *Political Science Quarterly*, 61:631 (December 1946).

[23] Loewenberg, *op. cit.*, p. 506.

[24] Bulletin 54, p. 52.

[25] Wallace E. Caldwell, *Social Forces*, 25:359 (March 1947).

tended the value hypothesis. This president boldly declared that the historian had a great opportunity for social service, because "the curve which he plots for the past inevitably projects itself into the future. He points the way . . . in an age of transition from laissez faire to a planned society in which we will either be ruled by a dictatorship or by a government democratically controlled. . . . The liberal neutral attitude, the approach to social evolution in terms of dispassionate behaviorism will no longer suffice. . . . The important thing is that we shall accept and endorse such controls as are essential for the preservation of our way of life." [26] Bulletin 54 did not venture so far, although the fears that it aroused did so.

The chapter on "Problems of Terminology in Historical Writing" took its special character from the discovery that historical practice was too individualistic to serve as a guide for defining even as few as 50 terms. Scholars who believe that historical terms are incapable of definition were inclined to doubt that this chapter provided material aid in the teaching and writing of history. But the Committee's belief that greater precision in the use of historical terms is a desirable goal was evidently widely shared. Numerous commentators welcomed, as steps toward clarification, Beard's note on the need for greater precision and Hook's 13 brief essays on meanings attributable to 21 primary terms. One scholar early prophesied: "since most historians in America are good children of the eighteenth-century Enlightenment, it seems likely that a substantial majority of them would accept in general Hook's position." [27]

The gratefully inclined termed this chapter "very useful" with special reference to the terms "change," "development," and "progress." [28] They variously described it as the "beginnings of a valuable and much needed task"; [29] "as cogent to the work of the historian as the terminology of a Bernheim or a Langlois and Seignobos"; [30] with the chapter on Propositions, as the "meatiest of the chapters." [31]

Other social scientists expressed their interest, approval, and criticism in their periodicals. The chapter on terminology "compressed an amazing quantity of sober sense into a small space"; with the Proposi-

[26] Conyers Read, "Social Responsibilities of the Historian," *American Historical Review*, 55:285, 283, 284 (January 1950).

[27] Brinton, *op. cit.*, p. 342.

[28] Michael Kraus, *Mississippi Valley Historical Review*, 33:327 (September 1946).

[29] Strong, *op. cit.*, p. 99.

[30] Harry E. Barnes, *American Sociological Review*, 12:360 (June 1947).

[31] Mood, *op. cit.*, p. 438.

tions it was "especially rewarding for all social scientists"; and "The utility of the Report in anthropological seminars and other advanced courses is obvious." [32] The attempt at definitions illustrating "the extreme difficulties arising from casual and varied uses of words . . . was certainly worth while," especially the definitions of cause and progress.[33] On the other hand, a reviewer for a periodical in one of the social sciences which historians sometimes find addicted to talking in strange tongues deplored what he conceived might become a call for "scientific jargon"; and to him the analysis of cause added little if anything to what the reader must have gained from Beale.[34] Yet another found Hook's treatment of causation "a model of clear and concise reasoning." [35]

Apparently scholars in the humanities also could find grist to their mill in this report; "the philosopher, no less than the historian, should find it most informative and suggestive throughout." [36] But the not surprising fact that Hook's material and some other wordings in the report were not in agreement on all points disturbed some of the philosophical brethren; the term "history-as-actuality" became a favorite bone of contention. Whereas Hook's presentation and the principle of relativist selection were interpreted to deny that history-as-actuality could be subject matter of historical knowledge, Beard said that historians "are bound" to be concerned with it and that against it "the abstractions of the humanistic sciences are to be checked for validity." [37] The idea of historical checking of humanistic sciences was repelled with some vigor: "Knowledge for a determinate context admits no comprehensive context-of-contexts known to historians by which to check either humanistic sciences or their own histories." [38]

Often it has been remarked that arguments between the United States and Great Britain are aggravated by the fact that they use the same language but attribute different meanings to identical words. Argument over Bulletin 54, at any rate, repeatedly rose from that universal failing, imprecision. The chapter comprising the 21 Propositions is another case in point. Striving for precision of terminology, the Committee weighed and reweighed every word, discussing at great

[32] Robert H. Lowie, *American Anthropologist*, 49:119 (January–March 1947).
[33] Caldwell, *op. cit.*, p. 359.
[34] E. R. Adair, *American Journal of Sociology*, 52:459 (March 1947).
[35] Robin M. Williams, Jr., *Rural Sociology*, 11:295 (September 1946).
[36] Arthur Child, *Ethics*, 57:310 (July 1947).
[37] Bulletin 54, p. 12.
[38] Edward W. Strong, *Philosophical Review*, 56:100 (January 1947).

length its multifarious meanings; and the final choice of a word hung upon its applicability to the broad concept that the group had in mind.

But when these words met the eyes of readers, the interpretation of each proposition hung upon the meaning that the particular reader assigned to those words in that context; the concept might be narrow or wide. It is not surprising, therefore, that some commentators opined that "honest" or "thoughtful" historians would quarrel with but few of the Propositions; while one critic both honest and thoughtful found the Propositions variously inconsistent, vague, confused, perplexing, overlapping, irreconcilable, and platitudinous! [39] Still other scholars, seeing broader and more useful possibilities of interpretation, thought that dissent would be "inevitable" on some, and debate would be needed. Debate did bloom in healthy vigor and in itself justified the publication of Bulletin 54 as helping to maintain a continuing clash of opposing doctrine.

Debate waxed hottest over two aspects stressed throughout the bulletin and summarized in the Propositions: over the warnings against unrecognized assumptions, and over the plea to adopt hypotheses as working tools.

Counsel on assumptions was summarized in Propositions VI, VII, and VIII. These asserted that schemes of reference influence all written or spoken history, and that historians by conscious clarification of thought and purpose should attempt to free themselves from the "bondage" of the subconscious, the routine, and the surreptitious. While few could be found to deny that "complete objectivity" was impossible, some mistakenly saw an implication that an approach toward greater objectivity was impossible, and this they declared was weak surrender to a negativist position.

It appeared that the report dealt "a devastating blow to the old concept and ideal of objectivity" [40] and ideals are not to be lightly lost. Among fears aroused by the report's stress upon the dangers in unconscious or unbridled use of one's frame of reference were apprehensions that all frames of reference would be held to be equally good

[39] W. Stull Holt, "An Evaluation of the Report on Theory and Practice in Historical Study," *Pacific Historical Review*, 18:236–238 (May 1949). This critic found the report a failure in its major effort, but "surely a glorious failure. No comparable challenge to the historians of America has been given unless it be" the address of Henry Adams to the American Historical Association in 1894 (p. 239).

[40] A. R. Newsome, *North Carolina Historical Review*, 24:119 (January 1947).

(a contention emphatically denied by a Committee member [41]), that the present would be overemphasized, and that history would be neglected in favor of philosophical speculation.[42]

The differences among historians on the importance of the frame of reference were further illustrated by the reactions of three other scholars, among many. One wrote that attributes of admirable historians include "attributes which somehow stand apart from the elements of time and place," and that emphasis on relativism "brings us no forwarder to a solution" [43] of the problem of defining the elements that make good history. Contrariwise, another declared that "everyone has values. It is impossible to elude them. They are there. We might just as well face them at once, bring them out in the open rather than have them reappear again through the back door or the cellar window." [44] Another scholar had "nothing but praise . . . for such points as the Committee's forthright emphasis on the inevitability of selection among facts and the need for making value premises explicit." [45]

The Propositions warned against some kinds of schemes of reference in particular; for example, Proposition IX cautions against accepting theological or philosophical absolutes as mandates for selecting data. A bothered historian demanded more explanation: "isn't Proposition VI itself an absolute of that philosophical school known as relativism?" [46] The answer was that the Committee advocated the opposite of a mandate; it advocated freeing oneself as far as possible from one's scheme of reference, a position sometimes summarized in the term "objective relativism." But there are almost innumerable kinds of relativists, and each historian willing to accept the designation chooses his own particular qualifying adjective.

One critic entered an earnest plea for the use of "Methods of Extending the Limits of Certainty," suggesting use of the analytical methods of physicists and semanticists with exclusion of what is immeasurable and with historical writing confined to specialists.[47] But

[41] Louis Gottschalk, remarks at session on "Present Problems in Historiography," American Historical Association Annual Meeting, Cleveland, December 28, 1947.

[42] Lynn M. Case, remarks at Cleveland session.

[43] Handlin, op. cit., pp. 540, 539.

[44] Loewenberg, remarks at Cleveland session.

[45] Williams, op. cit., p. 295.

[46] Holt, Pennsylvania Magazine of History, 72:82 (January 1948).

[47] James C. Malin, paper read at Cleveland session.

scientists as guides had no appeal to a commentator on this paper. "Historians are wiser than scientists," he said, for the former take care not to forget the historical importance of that which continues a long time; the only solution is "a return to a quest for wisdom instead of a quest for certainty." [48] It was observed that relativism was of service in the quest for certainty. "Once we have stamped finality as the great heresy for scholars, we can see the concept of the relativity of knowledge as a movement in the direction of greater objectivity." [49]

On two Propositions objections seemed almost nonexistent. Numbers x and xi which refused to abandon the term "cause," though warning of its limitations, had split the Committee six to two; but these Propositions did not split the profession, which in general agreed that it would be extremely difficult to devise workable substitutes for such terms as "cause" and "causality."

The gradations of welcome received by Bulletin 54 interested various commentators. One declared that it was "too much a revelation of fallibility to be welcome to some professional historians." [50] A general welcome among social scientists was envisaged by an economist who saw the "whole tenor" as an implicit "plea for collaboration in the social sciences" and found it "of interest and importance to any social scientist who ever has occasion to use historical data." [51] And who among them has not?

Among all the positions attributed to Bulletin 54 was one from which nobody could remove it: it flowed along in the stream of American development. The great achievements of the pioneers in "scientific" history were not denied; but the Committee believed it "no longer profitable for historians to claim that they merely record facts in an objective order determined by inductive logic." They were fully aware of the hazards involved in trying to make historical writing "an instrument for the intelligent control of the future by making it a systematic (and *really* 'scientific') study of the uniformities of human behavior." But they believed the attempt should be made. "Their position is, of course, quite in the tradition of the pioneers. Had they gone over to dogma, prophesying, consolation, or despair, to any recipe for a ready-made faith, then, indeed, they would have made a break

[48] Stanley Pargellis, comments on "Methods of Extending the Limits of Certainty," Cleveland session.

[49] Willson H. Coates, "Relativism and the Use of Hypothesis in History" (paper read at Cleveland session), *Journal of Modern History*, 21:24 (March 1949).

[50] David S. Berkowitz, *The World in Books* (December 1946).

[51] Bert F. Hoselitz, *Journal of Political Economy*, 55:388 (August 1947).

with the past of historical writing in America." [52] As it was, a number of scholars expressed a keen desire for more historiographical efforts.

RECENT SHIFTS OF EMPHASIS IN AMERICAN HISTORIOGRAPHY

The "climate of opinion" during the work on this second bulletin has of course shifted somewhat from that which harbored Bulletin 54. This is not to claim rashly that entirely new trends have startled the historical guild during the past eight years. But it is fair to say that certain changes of emphasis have been carried farther forward in the realm of thought and action. Of these sharpened emphases space permits mention here of but five—each fertile in itself and all together proof of vigorous animation in historiography.

Foremost in its potentialities is the growing emphasis on *fraternization or amalgamation with other disciplines.* As more historians reject occupational isolation, admit some sharing of methodological problems, and assume the possibility of mutual re-enforcement, they are found at work with other scholars in many fields. More historians are now treading the pioneering trail of cooperative exploration with social psychologists, social anthropologists, and sociologists; emboldened by foundation grants for an occasional "Behavioral Council," adherents of these four disciplines experiment variously. Community studies offer one focus for such experiments; where the community is studied as a whole, interdisciplinary cooperation avoids some of the distortions common under disciplinary fragmentation.[53] Another focus has been found in the concept of entrepreneurship, defined broadly as the function of initiating and administering change through business units; sociology, anthropology, social psychology, and economics have all proved indispensable for an adequate understanding of the historical changes in this social function.[54] And the conditions and processes of economic development, conceived as involving changes in many non-

[52] Brinton, *op. cit.,* p. 342.

[53] One experiment of this type is the "Norristown Project" at the University of Pennsylvania—an attempt to ascertain the interrelations between industrialization and social change in one community over a 50-year period, 1900–1950.

[54] This, at least, has been the experience of the Research Center in Entrepreneurial History at Harvard University, founded in 1948. For a sample of the work of this Research Center see its journal, *Explorations in Entrepreneurial History,* and William Miller, ed., *Men in Business* (Cambridge: Harvard University Press, 1952). Emphasis on the historical significance of business enterprise has been greatly facilitated by the multiplying histories of specific businesses in which N. S. B. Gras, Henrietta M. Larson, and others in the Harvard Graduate School of Business Administration have been active.

economic aspects of culture, have proved equally fruitful as a focus for cross-disciplinary research.[55]

Disciplinary mergers also flourish in "area studies" whereby increasing numbers of university historians associate more or less actively with political scientists, linguists, economists, anthropologists, geographers, and other professional groups in studies of such regions as the Near East, South Asia, Southeast Asia, the Far East, or the Atlantic Community. Somewhat similarly, "American Civilization" programs increasingly bring historians into joint activity with professors of literature, sociology, fine arts, anthropology, and philosophy. Amalgamation often has failed to achieve the effectiveness that was hoped for, and teamwork on the whole still remains more honored in the breach than the observance; but it gives evidence of growth and of widening awareness of the broadening problems, methods, and scope of history.

Among the other emphases of the past few years, on a lesser scale of significance, the following four are especially important: [56]

1. Diplomatic history increasingly emphasizes an international interpretation of America's past, whether writers be of the pro-Roosevelt school of Langer and Gleason [57] or the anti-Roosevelt school of Beard [58] and Tansill; [59] this emphasis seems almost inevitable at this postwar, cold-war juncture as the United States shoulders world-wide responsibilities.

2. Achievements of builders of national might, such as the Rockefellers and Fords, are pressed forward for emphasis by Allan Nevins.[60]

[55] In this connection the work of the Research Center in Economic Development and Cultural Change at the University of Chicago is especially relevant for historians.

[56] Cogent summaries of these trends are found in *Social Science Frontiers: Annual Proceedings of the Middle States Council for the Social Studies, 1951–1952*, 49:9–61; to Eric Goldman's "Fresh Winds in Historiography" (pp. 19–24), this writer acknowledges particular indebtedness. The volume contains also correlative comment on labor agreements, political science, economics, social psychology, and geography by Stuart Chase, F. Morstein Marx, S. Howard Patterson, M. Brewster Smith, and Frank E. Sorenson.

[57] William L. Langer and John H. Gleason, *The Challenge to Isolation* (New York: Harper & Brothers, 1952); they had a small staff to help on this monumental work.

[58] Charles A. Beard, *President Roosevelt and the Coming of the War, 1941* (New Haven: Yale University Press, 1948).

[59] Charles C. Tansill, *Back Door to War: The Roosevelt Foreign Policy, 1933–1941* (Chicago: H. Regnery Co., 1952).

[60] Speech at Stanford University, August 5, *New York Times*, August 6, 1951; *Ford: The Times, the Man, the Company*, in collaboration with Ernest D. Hill (New York: Charles Scribner's Sons, 1954).

In order to deal with the appalling plethora of the relevant documentation, he has developed the art of working with trained assistants who mine mountains of historical ore and run the ore through a furnace of critical examination before final refinement by the supervisory historian, enabling the latter constructively to exploit whole ranges of historical resources.

3. A concomitant emphasis calls for stress upon the conservative element in United States traditions and upon conservative leadership. This emphasis was boldly advocated by S. E. Morison in his 1950 presidential address before the American Historical Association.[61]

4. Emphasis on minorities as such, involving a sharper focus than the earlier studies of immigration in general, evidences further the inclination of some historians to accept more varied demands upon their skills.[62]

These and other turns of emphasis have been penetrating historical soil, aerating it, and stimulating the growth of historiographical upshoots. Bulletin 54 has been effective in at least three respects. It has stimulated considerable thought and endless discussion from which the guild could profit. It has called forth some constructive criticism, also a source of profit. It has encouraged a demand for more reports, proving anew that historians have a large capacity for continuing self-examination.

The scholars who have expressed hopes for more reports have asked for enough varieties of content to keep committees busy for a very long time. But in particular a more positive type of report now seems to be desired. A negative emphasis had seemed to predominate in Bulletin 54, perhaps partly because of its numerous emphatic warnings against such dangers as unrecognized assumptions, facile use of "cause," imprecise terminology, dogmatism, reliance upon historical "constants," and superficial analogies between historical and scientific methods.

[61] Samuel E. Morison, "Faith of a Historian," *American Historical Review,* 56:272–273 (January 1951). Along this line are two volumes published in the same year: Bernard E. Brown, *American Conservatives: The Political Thought of Francis Lieber and John W. Burgess* (New York: Columbia University Press, 1951) and Robert G. McCloskey, *American Conservatism in the Age of Enterprise: A Study of William Graham Sumner, Stephen J. Field and Andrew Carnegie* (Cambridge: Harvard University Press, 1951).

[62] See Oscar Handlin, *The Uprooted* (Boston: Little, Brown and Company, 1951); and Carl F. Wittke, *We Who Built America: The Saga of the Immigrant* (2nd ed.; New York: Prentice-Hall, 1946).

The need for such warnings was not denied, but more "practical guidance" was called for; subsequent reports "might well devote less attention to facts and causes and more to such inclusive historiographical conceptions as periodization, climate of opinion, and culture pattern." [63] "Relativism has made value theory crucial to the success of historical scholarship. A hallowed principle of the historian's creed and a cardinal assumption of all learning must therefore be reappraised; its opposite must be restored to a level of respectability sufficient at least to make it entertainable." [64]

Among other areas suggested for further exploration in subsequent historiographical studies, the following were prominently mentioned: more analysis of assumptions controlling scholars in very recent years; more emphasis on attributes other than those of time and place; broader analysis of behavior to provide clearer insight in making hypotheses; more emphasis upon the local community as the seedbed of history; imperative need for a higher level of intellectual performance; reinforcement of historic concepts of such moral values as cooperation, freedom, and strength; definition of the elements present in historical writing that has stood the test of time; more attention to literary values and the avoidance of extra-erudite terminology; techniques for handling the staggering plethora of data; evaluations of the potentialities of cooperative research; a more definite and positive statement of the implications of general reciprocity in use of concepts prevailing in the thinking of historians and their fellow social scientists.

From these many and varied suggestions the present Committee decided to select an area of inquiry which appeared to be not only of contemporary interest but also of considerable long-range significance: exploration of how historians and other social scientists can better attain profitable intellectual cooperation, through more effective knowledge and use of ideas and methods dominant in the various social sciences. Historians can profit by such knowledge and use, but it is not a one-way relationship—they can teach much as well.

This report represents part of the results of the Committee's investigations—part, but not all, for no printed document can fully reflect the process of re-education that an attempt to analyze social science approaches makes necessary. The members of the Committee, it need

[63] Stow Persons, *William and Mary Quarterly*, 3(3rd series):602 (October 1946).
[64] Loewenberg, "Some Problems Raised by Historical Relativism" (paper read at Cleveland session), *Journal of Modern History*, 21:23 (March 1949).

hardly be said, make no claim to significant originality, far less to finality, in their conclusions. They offer this report for the consideration of their fellow historians in the hope that, like its predecessor, it will stimulate serious thought, fruitful discussion, and constructive criticism. Thereby historiography may move on, in the building tradition of the pioneers.

2 HISTORY AMONG THE SOCIAL SCIENCES: NATURE AND PURPOSE OF THE REPORT

The present report of the Committee on Historiography, like its predecessor, Bulletin 54, presents suggestions for more inclusive approaches to the study of history. It forms a supplement to the earlier report, for it seeks to carry out the recommendations of the previous committee: to deal with the problems involved in making effective use of social science concepts and social science methods in historical interpretation. Unlike its predecessor, however, this report is primarily concerned with substantive issues of method and analysis.

This report, although concerned with methods, is not a prescription designed to guide the research of individual historians. The essays which follow are efforts to extend the boundaries of historical thought, to widen the scope of historical investigation, to sharpen historical perspectives, and to clarify historical purposes. They are written in the belief that the enterprise of learning is a cooperative one, and that the advancement of learning requires constant reappraisal and refinement of its methods, objectives, and results. Concern for method is not simply a discipline; it is basic to every discipline. Whether called logic, philosophy, or scientific method, scholarship can be no better than its tools, instruments, or techniques. The use of knowledge is the purpose of scholarship; the assessment of the instruments of scholarship is a vital part of it. Scholarship exists for the sake of life, and the instruments of reason are the life of learning.

While the members of the Committee are appreciative of semantics as an aid to reflection, they have not undertaken a semantic study. Nor have they sought to add to the language of scholarship by coining new words or endowing old phrases with novel meanings. They have simply tried to reaffirm an ancient proposition: that history is the study of mankind in *all* its bewildering variety. Accordingly, this report is devoted to an exposition of methods and concepts now current in various branches of the social sciences. It is hoped that historians, to a considerable extent already aware of their relevance, will make larger use of them.

THE GROWTH OF KNOWLEDGE

Concepts, whether in history, physics, or psychology, do not remain in *status quo*. Every intellectual formulation is a formulation after one analysis and before another. Concepts, like the data they are fashioned to organize and explain, are themselves refashioned. Since cultural and conceptual change are interactive, changes in ideas alter culture and changes in culture alter ideas. New data, new methods, new insights produce new knowledge and new understandings.

Knowledge of course is cumulative, but ideas, concepts, and hypotheses develop at different rates of growth in different areas of thought. The rate of change varies in individual sciences as well as among individual scientists. No over-all hypothesis unifies scholarship. Concepts chosen for illustration by the present Committee were chosen for their suggestiveness. Practitioners in the various areas from which they were selected are not necessarily in agreement with all the hypotheses employed in their own fields. We have selected representative hypotheses, not universal axioms. Indeed the Committee is persuaded that no such axioms exist. We share the belief with many of our colleagues in other disciplines that concepts are instrumental. They are formulated for the purpose of enlarging human understanding and are themselves subject to growth and change. They are procedural rules, not invariant principles. The criterion of selection has been fertility, not consensus.

As historians we are impressed with the inferences that can legitimately be drawn from the history of thought. It is virtually accurate to say that the more general the hypothesis and the more widely it is held, the less it is likely to stimulate deviations from accepted standards. If a hypothesis is broadly diffused, it rarely serves the function of intellectual innovation. The theory of evolution, for example, has been too long in general currency to stimulate by itself fresh exploration in biology and kindred sciences. When biological evolution was an "outrageous hypothesis," it was a seminal hypothesis. Biological research is no longer initiated by Darwinian dialectics, but by the specific and controversial hypotheses in heredity, cytology, and microbiological analysis. The concept of culture, highly suggestive in the days of Tylor and Wissler, is not the sophisticated series of concepts employed by Malinowski, Kroeber, and Kluckhohn. And the more complex the concept, the greater the likelihood of disagreement.

Diversity is the earned increment of scholarship. Sigmund Freud gave intellectual direction to modern psychology, but his influence produced a variety of psychological schools. What is true of psychology is equally true of sociology, economics, and political science. Locke's concept of political power is not Rousseau's. Nor do the speculations of either conform to the clashing theories of group interests as developed by modern research. Disagreement is often a concomitant of intellectual vitality.

The purpose of the Committee on Historiography is not only to provoke further discussion and to define differences, but also to advance the investigation of methods, issues, and meanings. The report is addressed in the first instance to young historians who are in the process of working out their conception of the nature and functions of history. But it is also addressed to all historians concerned with the development of history and engaged in the professional training of advanced students. The essays comprising this report are not designed to serve as a manual of historical practice, nor do they emulate earlier attempts at formal surveys of social science methods.[1] Rather, they examine certain social science methods that may be of use to historians, in order to indicate their possibilities as well as their limitations, and to suggest grounds for believing that further progress in historical study might derive from the use of such methods.

ORGANIZATION OF THE REPORT

In seeking an effective way of presenting its views, the Committee considered various expedients. An initial attempt to survey the areas, problems, and particular analytical techniques of each of the social sciences was abandoned. The Committee also abandoned, after a considerable amount of work had been done, a case study of the use of certain social science concepts in history, dealing specifically with the Civil War period,[2] for it soon became obvious that an adequately informative and concrete demonstration would require a substantial book. Exploratory essays appeared to be a more fruitful device and this plan was adopted: a survey of concepts and viewpoints in the social sciences (Chapter 3) is followed by discussions of social science analysis of historical materials (Chapter 4), of the nature and analysis of his-

[1] See, for example, Stuart A. Rice, ed., *Methods in Social Science: A Case Book* (Chicago: University of Chicago Press, 1931); William F. Ogburn and Alexander Goldenweiser, eds., *The Social Sciences and Their Interrelations* (Boston: Houghton Mifflin Company, 1927); Harry E. Barnes, *The New History and the Social Sciences* (New York: Century Co., 1925); and the relevant articles in the *Encyclopaedia of the Social Sciences*.

[2] Prepared by Bert James Loewenberg, in consultation with S. H. Brockunier, Shepard B. Clough, and Thomas C. Cochran.

torical change (Chapter 5), and of the use of theory and hypotheses and various other problems of method (Chapter 6). The Committee also decided to include a critique of current practice as reflected in conventional American historical syntheses, suggesting its limitations in terms of the approaches employed in some of the other social sciences (Chapter 7).

As contrasted with conventional historical syntheses, the conception of history used throughout this report is based on a wider use of ideas and concepts in other social sciences. The Committee presents its view as but one way of approaching the study of history. The Committee has not passed judgment on the "legitimacy" of alternative approaches. To do so is clearly beyond the competence of any committee. The function of this report is neither to exhort nor to adjudicate, but to explore.

That history can be regarded as a social science needs little argument. Historians have long been aware of their responsibilities as social scientists. They have consistently affirmed the necessity of analyzing historical data rigorously. For some generations, too, the practice as well as the philosophy of historians has reflected the scientific spirit; historical studies that exhibit modes of thinking directly traceable to a social science viewpoint are now common. A work such as Bulletin 54, for example, embodying the group judgment of representative historians, could not have appeared had not history in the United States attained a certain degree of maturity as a social science. The problem that remains is one of making more explicit as a matter of practice the status already recognized in principle—of making investigation more penetrating, analysis more precise, and demonstration more rigorous. This is a problem that history, in company with other sciences, has always to face.

The material contained in this report falls logically into two parts: a discussion of the relevance for the historian of methods of inquiry developed in the other social disciplines; and a discussion of the nature of history itself as a social science. So conceived, history involves its own distinctive problems and demands the development of distinctive techniques of research and interpretation for their solution.

In connection with the first group of problems the Committee had the benefit of a series of conferences with representatives of each of several social science disciplines. To these scholars the Committee is deeply indebted; its work would hardly have been possible without their cooperation. The conferences were highly illuminating and provided the conceptual data on which much of the material in this report,

and particularly in Chapter 3, was initially based. Moreover, these conferences substantiated the belief of the Committee that there were important convergences in the various approaches of the social sciences. For example, history and anthropology converge in the analysis of culture, and all fields of social science exhibit convergences in the analysis of groups. The Committee concluded that the convergences are manifest; that possibilities for their creative employment are not being fully exploited; and that they can be.

The Committee considered the feasibility of identifying areas of inquiry that, although intensively studied in these allied fields, have usually been neglected in written history. Among these are the changing structure of the family and the relationships between culture and personality. But it was always apparent that a systematic examination of areas of research in the social sciences would be a formidable undertaking, while a cursory survey would be of slight value. As adequate descriptions of the particular methods and techniques of each of the nonhistorical social sciences were readily available, the Committee did not consider it worth while to catalogue social science methods. It therefore undertook the exploration of convergences and substantial areas of agreement among the social sciences, and of suggestions as to how they can be utilized in historical research.

The conferences with experts from other fields proved highly informative, also, in connection with the second group of problems, those concerning the nature of history and its interpretation as a social science. It became evident at an early stage that history must be regarded as unique among social sciences in one important respect, namely that its focus of interest is explicitly the analysis of change over time. Other social sciences, of course, include the analysis of change within their field of reference. But in no other branch of social science inquiry is the element of time so inextricably involved in data, methods, and interpretation as it is in history. In the opinion of the Committee, since many social science methods are not explicitly designed to deal with temporal sequences and processes, the use of such methods for historical purposes presents major difficulties.

These considerations strongly suggested to the Committee that the task of modifying and adapting methods developed in other social sciences, in order that the most effective use may be made of them in history, is one that historians cannot delegate or expect to have performed for them by others. There are no ready-made solutions, no devices that can be taken over without careful scrutiny, experiment, and adaptation. Ordinarily the expert in an allied field is not competent to prescribe for the historian the concrete operations by which he can deal with the problems presented by historical data.

The Committee believes that collaboration between historians and other social scientists should be cultivated as effectively as possible. It believes that the process of mutual education that takes place when historians and persons trained in other disciplines attack a given problem from several different approaches, maintaining close communication with each other and striving to overcome the many deep-seated barriers to mutual understanding, holds great promise for the future and is always to be encouraged. It seems safe to predict, however, that historians individually must find out what data and what methods of social science can enlarge the scope and meaning of their research. They must determine for themselves what they must modify, and what they must devise independently to meet their own requirements.

PROCESS OF HISTORICAL RESEARCH

Research in history as in all science should begin with that frequently overlooked but vital step in the advancement of learning: the recognition that there is something to be explained. Bulletin 54 emphasized that the problems that historians recognize and regard as "basic" vary from generation to generation: "In 1944 the United States is not what it was in 1927. Hence the historian, facing the problem of selecting those facts in the American past that seem 'basic' for 1944, will not be able to make just the same selection that he made in 1927." [3] The meaning of the past is seen in the present; and as the present changes, so does the meaning we see in the past.

There is another reason why the problems examined by historians will alter in the future. Historians of different generations will select different sets of problems for examination, not only because their immediate interests (as affected by the contemporary conjuncture of world events) change, but also because they will be able to accept certain propositions as tentatively established with a degree of probability sufficient to warrant their acceptance. The accumulation of knowledge, the ability to build with confidence upon foundations solidly established, is the prospect held out by greater communication between history and the other social sciences.

What is the process by which this prospect may be realized? What

[3] Randall and Haines, p. 18.

precepts or rules of procedure must the historian follow to contribute to this end? The following chapters are concerned with these questions, and there is no need to anticipate here what will be discussed at length later. It may be helpful, however, to set the discussion in proper perspective. Concretely, what difference does greater awareness of current concepts in other social sciences make to the individual historian, engaged in research, writing, teaching, and thinking about history?

Any historian who employs these concepts in the hope of finding an easy solution to his research problems is certain to be disappointed. There is no such thing as *the* social science method. There are more complex approaches and unfamiliar points of view, and there are certain techniques of inquiry that have been found useful in many disciplines. But there are no neat, well-formulated social science methods that can be learned and applied without scrutiny; and no social science concept either implies or involves any deviation from the strict rules of procedure that are the hallmark of sound historical research. The function of these various concepts is to aid the investigator to discriminate: to decide upon the basis of more inclusive and more sharply defined criteria what is significant and what is not; to appraise the evidence more systematically; and to evaluate the sequences of change more subtly.

The fundamental problem of historical study is the analysis of change over time. Some social sciences have found it possible, in general, to push the problem of time into the background. The analysis of "dynamics," of change and development, has only recently been recognized again as a problem of the first priority by economists, who have long been content to devote the greater part of their ingenuity and energy to the elaboration of what are termed static models. However justifiable or convenient such a procedure may be in other disciplines, historians cannot adopt it. Their data are events that are related by their position in time, no matter in what other ways they may be related. That is why every historical event, however similar to others, is in some respects unique. For historians, therefore, the element of time can never be a somewhat inconvenient and unmanageable "fourth dimension" to be introduced almost as an afterthought in the final stages of the analysis. It must be *in* the analysis from the beginning.

In all science the purpose of research is knowledge, the understanding of relationships. In historical research such understanding involves a great deal more than the mere arrangement of events in the order in which they occurred in time. A chronicle gives information but not understanding. For the latter, one must discover the ways in which events are interrelated beyond their relations of temporal sequence or coincidence. In particular one must discover how they are related as cause and consequence. This involves the selection of events, their arrangement in logical as well as temporal patterns, and their ordering in rank according to some criteria of significance. It involves, in a word, the use of concepts and hypotheses.

Sometimes historians state their theories explicitly, in which case it is not very difficult to check their results and to decide what has been demonstrated and what has not. More often, however, the theories are left implicit, taken for granted, or simply not known; in this case the charitable are wont to refer to them as insights, the critical as intuitions. The historian may gain from his more intensive consideration of concepts and methods in other social sciences a more explicit use of theory. He will place greater reliance on theory in the form of concepts by which to organize his data; he will utilize hypotheses derived from theory to guide the search for evidence and to suggest possible interpretations; and he may obtain from theory the criteria that enable him to decide when a proposition has been adequately demonstrated. Without adequate use of theory historical study cannot attain its full potential. It is the use of theory that permits us to hope that in history, as in other sciences, the results of research may become increasingly cumulative.

If every historical event were literally unique, history as science would be inconceivable. The historian would then merely record the events of the past; no generalizations whatsoever would be possible; history as actuality would *mean* nothing; and any attempt to *understand* the past would be entirely futile. But no historical event can be utterly and completely unique. Otherwise it would be impossible for us to say anything about it, or even to apprehend it as an event. As soon as we recognize anything, whether it is a historical event or a physical object, we recognize it because it has certain characteristics in common with other events and objects. Each historical event is unique, to be sure, in some respects; but it is also similar in other respects to other historical events.

When similar events are placed in the same class and the class is given a name, we have made use of a concept. And whenever we use that concept we refer to the common characteristics because of which we have grouped these events into one class. A theory is essentially a set of propositions that assert that certain concepts are interrelated in certain ways. The group of concepts is sometimes called a conceptual scheme. The propositions that tell how they are related are definitions, postulates, or hypotheses.

The function of theory in history is precisely the same as in other fields of inquiry: to suggest problems, to provide categories for organizing data, to supply hypotheses by which various interpretations of the data may be tested, and to lay down criteria of proof. No theory can provide the investigator with "answers." On the contrary, theory provides the investigator with questions. The most a theory in its initial stages can do is to suggest tentative working hypotheses, once a problem has been isolated. These hypotheses must then be tested against the evidence. If the test is successful, then we have something more than a hypothesis; we have instead a generalization which holds **with a certain degree** of probability and which can serve as a provisional explanation. If the test is unsuccessful, then our hypothesis and perhaps the whole conceptual structure from which our hypothesis was derived must be questioned.

Hypotheses, then, are devices, means of exploring data. This particular aspect of scientific method can be a source of misunderstanding not only among historians but also among social scientists in various fields. Unless the individual reporting his research is careful to make the distinction, a generalization stated as a hypothesis and a generalization stated as a conclusion look very much alike. This is particularly likely to be the case when, as in history, research is reported in literary form. Unless the context makes it clear, there is no means of telling whether a statement such as "The larger the market, the greater the degree of specialization" is to be construed as hypothesis, assumption, or conclusion. In strict logic of course all are hypotheses, though with different degrees of probability; but in the reporting of specific research there is a vast difference between them.

If this difference were always made explicit, which would be highly desirable, one might encounter less frequently a typical objection to social science method in history, that it encourages too great facility in generalization and obscures the uniqueness of historical events.[4]

___

[4] The proposition that all historical phenomena are unique and the corollary that no general statements whatsoever can be made about historical processes have been explicitly advanced by certain German historiographers and, implicitly, underlie many objections to a social science approach. This position appears to rest in part upon faulty logic and in part upon a semantic confusion over the term "unique." From one point of view it is no doubt true that the historical process is unique;

When social science methods are used carelessly or irresponsibly, there is weight to this charge. More frequently, however, it arises from a misunderstanding of how hypotheses are used. Many social science inquiries are designed and executed purely as tests of hypotheses. In such an inquiry it is essential that the hypotheses to be tested be made explicit at an early stage of the investigation. This does not mean that the investigator has prejudged the issue; it does mean that he has brought his insights and "hunches" out into the open and reduced them to empirically testable propositions. By doing so he has simplified not only his own task, but also that of the reader and of any investigator who wishes to check his findings.

The erection of hypotheses, or the framing of questions that can be answered positively or negatively from the material under examination, is not, of course, confined to any one stage of the analysis. The stage of research at which such questions can profitably be posed varies from the beginning to the end. Tentative initial hypotheses must be modified in the light of the evidence and then tested against new evidence. The scholar well versed in a special field may have many tentative presuppositions which he should commit to writing at the start and subject to careful checking. In dealing with problems on which a considerable amount of research has been done, the experience of previous investigators may provide helpful models, but the procedures used should always be thoroughly scrutinized. At the other extreme is the situation where social science knowledge suggests the examination of a particular aspect of behavior but offers few clues as to the probable findings. As a general rule, however, problems should be defined and hypotheses developed as early in the analysis as possible. *Ad hoc* hypotheses, drawn up only after the evidence has been selected, are like the results of an uncontrolled experiment: they can serve only as particular explanations of particular data and can contribute little to the cumulative growth of knowledge, unless used as the starting point for more systematic investigation and testing.

There are two well-recognized general ways of using hypotheses in

---

but from the point of view of the social scientist every historical event shares traits with other historical events of the same general type. Careless use of social science methods may indeed justify criticism that important variables have been ignored. It is untrue, however, that social science is not concerned with the variations that make up singular differences. Furthermore, consideration of the time element makes it necessary to regard singular events as parts of processes, and a process is more than the sum of unique happenings.

social science inquiry. The steps are the same in each, but they are taken in a different order. In the first, the investigator sets out with the explicit purpose of testing a theory or conventional interpretation. Instead of starting with a set of observations (the historian's "primary sources") and then selecting a theory or hypothesis that seems likely to assist in explaining them, he begins with a hypothesis derived by inference from a theory and then searches for evidence that will prove or disprove that hypothesis and thus support or cast doubt upon the theory.

This procedure is not uncommon in historical research, but it is frequently attempted unsystematically and without proper appreciation of its limitations. Not all historical theories and generalizations can be tested empirically in the manner just described. There is an important distinction between operational and nonoperational theories. An operational theory is one that is stated in such a way that it can conceivably be proved false by reference to empirical evidence. Many historical theories, however, are not of this type and are not susceptible to direct empirical testing. This is particularly true of theories that employ metaphorical or incompletely defined concepts, since the empirical data to which such concepts are supposed to refer cannot be unambiguously determined.

A historian confronted with a nonoperational theory may evaluate it in terms of its internal logical consistency and of its general suggestiveness, but he cannot undertake to test it empirically unless he can devise operational equivalents for the concepts that the theory employs. For this reason many transcendental "theories of history" and many general interpretations of the nature of historical change are invulnerable to empirical refutation, although particular "translations" of these theories in terms of specified data can of course be tested in the usual way. Historical literature would be the poorer if deprived of the writings of such men as Spengler or Toynbee, but their theoretical structures should not be taken as examples of the use of social science methods. Only theories stated in operational terms, from which testable hypotheses can be unambiguously derived, can be handled by the methods of social science.

To set up a hypothesis for testing and then search for relevant evidence does not imply "making out a case" for that hypothesis. Negative findings, indicating that the hypothesis in question does not fit the evidence or fits only loosely, leaving considerable discrepancies still to be explained, are much more likely than positive findings and certainly no less valuable. Such negative conclusions, however, often do not find their way into print. There seems to be a human tendency to favor "proved" propositions. This tends to produce an erroneous impression of the ease and certainty with which scientific advance takes place. A few "case histories" of actual research in the social sciences, to parallel those in the natural sciences made by Conant and others, would soon dispel such notions.[5]

In historical research the process of inquiry ordinarily begins, not with testing hypotheses deduced from a general theory, but with a problem of interpretation presented by a certain body of empirical material. Whether in the natural or the social sciences, the procedure is the same. Confronted with such a problem, the investigator draws up a series of tentative working hypotheses, derived from his general knowledge of phenomena of this type and his familiarity with relevant theoretical developments, and then proceeds to test these hypotheses against his observations. Here again negative findings are of the utmost importance; indeed, certain historians stress the use of general concepts as a means of bringing out the unique aspects of the phenomena with which they deal, by emphasizing such findings or the inevitably imperfect fit of *any* general concept to the particular historical phenomenon.

Still a third type of inquiry, slightly different in nature, is applicable in cases where two or more theories have been devised to explain the same set of observations. Both theories are internally consistent and both give explanations which, if not complete, are at least valid within limits; yet they rest on incompatible assumptions. The problem in cases of this kind is either to disprove one of the theories or, more frequently, to reconcile them by the development of a more general theory that will include them both as special cases.

This type of problem is common in historical research. The contradictions between different theories of the "causes" of the Civil War, discussed at length in Bulletin 54, are a well-known example. Some of these theories are internally consistent and, given the author's basic assumptions, completely logical. Some of them provide interpretations that are highly plausible and that satisfactorily explain large segments of the data. They differ in that they are derived from different conceptual schemes and utilize different implicit theories of historical causation. *The problem is not to prove one right and the*

[5] See, for example, James B. Conant, *On Understanding Science* (New Haven: Yale University Press, 1947).

*others wrong, but to develop a more general explanation in which each
partial explanation will have its proper place.* Mere addition cannot
resolve them. It is necessary to develop a broader conceptual framework
from which "partial theories" can be systematically derived and in
terms of which they can be related to one another. Differences between
the preferences of different investigators, between what each regards as
causally significant, may then be seen in their true logical nature,
namely as the differences inherent in a set of tentative working
hypotheses which are to be tested for adequacy. The final explanation
will in all probability represent a systematic synthesis of a large number
of partial explanations.[6]

Problems of this nature are theoretical problems. They are soluble,
if soluble at all, by well-tried social science methods. They are not
necessarily irresolvable contradictions inherent in the nature of historical research. In other fields of inquiry this type of inconsistency,
when frankly recognized and investigated, has frequently led to fruitful
advances.[7]

In subsequent chapters problems involved in the use of concepts
and hypotheses in historical research are discussed in some detail. The
discussion may give the impression that the methods involved are more
abstract, more mechanical, or more complicated than is actually the
case. It may be prudent, therefore, to cite at this point one of Bridgman's obiter dicta: "I am not one of those who hold that there is a
scientific method as such. The scientific method, as far as it is a
method, is nothing more than doing one's damnedest with one's mind,
no holds barred."[8] A willingness to "do one's damnedest with one's
mind," however, is no excuse for waste motion. Some ways are obviously
more efficient than others. The methodological discussions in ex-
positions of the concepts and techniques of the various social sciences
are essentially discussions of how certain intellectual processes which
historians have always used, albeit unconsciously and uncritically, may
be made more rigorous and more predictable in their results.

[6] Another way of attacking the problem would be to select another case and test
the various partial theories against it, since the implication is that the relations
alleged to hold in one case should hold generally under similar circumstances.

[7] Einstein's work is a familiar example in the natural sciences; see Lincoln
Barnett, *The Universe and Dr. Einstein* (New York: New American Library of
World Literature, 1952). A more modest illustration in the social sciences is James
S. Duesenberry's revision of the theory of consumer behavior; see his *Income, Saving,
and the Theory of Consumer Behavior* (Cambridge: Harvard University Press, 1949).

[8] P. W. Bridgman, "The Prospect for Intelligence," *Yale Review,* 34:450 (March
1945); quoted by Conant, *op. cit.,* p. 115n.

INTERDISCIPLINARY COOPERATION

The development and application of the concepts and techniques of other social sciences in historical study require more frequent and continuous communication between historians and other social scientists. This can hardly be a one-sided process; and there is ample reason to believe that the nonhistorical social sciences have as much to gain from cooperation with historians as historians have from cooperation with social scientists. In strict logic the only evidence available to any social scientist, no matter what his specialty, is historical evidence. Yet social scientists in general have shown little awareness of the rich field of exploration that recorded history offers them, and have in many instances signally failed to grapple with the analysis of temporal processes. Further, the nonhistorical social sciences are essentially analytical disciplines and advance more by that approach than by synthesis; in historical study, on the other hand, the problem of final synthesis can never be avoided for long. Cooperation among the disciplines clearly promises benefit to all parties.

While it is easy to recommend interdisciplinary cooperation, it is difficult to achieve it. Certainly few who have made the attempt are likely to underestimate the difficulties. Cross-sterilization, as well as cross-fertilization, is a real possibility. Nor are the difficulties eased by emphasizing the barriers to communication imposed by technical vocabularies and "jargon," as is commonly done. Such barriers exist, but circumventing them involves an understanding of why they exist. If it were merely a matter of a specialist in one discipline acquiring a working knowledge of the terms used by a colleague in another, a few weeks of serious application would suffice. Unfortunately the situation is considerably more complicated. The barriers between the disciplines have grown up not through oversight nor merely as a by-product of university administration; they seem to have made it easier for the members of particular disciplines to perform some useful functions, such as setting and maintaining standards of workmanship. These functions are recognized and approved, but other by-products, which are seldom explicitly formulated, seem to be related more to matters of prestige and authority.

Barriers to mutual understanding are more than linguistic. There are conventional misapprehensions that malign the historian as well as his fellow social scientists. Certain historians find the generalizations of nonhistorical social scientists somewhat shocking. Impressed with the uniqueness of the historical fact, these historical scholars recoil from conclusions that seem to disregard the special and the particular. Some social scientists, on the other hand, entertain reservations about the historian and his method. Their image of the historian is equally distorted. He is a hunter after the fact, but he appears seldom to be concerned with the concept of a fact. Such critics regard the role of the historian as one defined by himself: the discoverer of "what really happened." But they affect amazement that as such he seldom conceptualizes in accordance with the processes of science, and appears to shun the patient routine of hypothesis, test, and new hypothesis. For them, he does not seem to understand analysis; he is too easily content to depict the past instead of raising questions about what the record reveals. Any serious appraisal of scholarship must reckon with such misapprehensions. The remedy, needless to say, does not lie wholly with historians. There are historians who do not understand what social scientists are trying to do and there are social scientists who have no sense of history.

Greater use by historians of the concepts of other social sciences entails not a redefinition of the purposes of history, but a reorientation of interest, a reconsideration of what is possible, and a re-examination of procedure. As a practical matter it involves a greater degree of cooperation and intercommunication between the historical profession and the other social science disciplines. This can be carried on at several different levels. The task facing the historical profession as a whole is that of integrating its research with the work being done in the nonhistorical social sciences to the end that greater understanding of how men and societies change and develop may be achieved. This must be a long and difficult process, to which it is hoped that this report will make some contribution. But to achieve interdisciplinary cooperation in practice is a matter for the individual historian, and for him fine words and lofty aims are not enough. At this level interdisciplinary cooperation means, simply, that people from different disciplines should work together on shared tasks. The Committee believes that the extension of this practice, which seems to be increasingly common in American universities, offers the most encouraging prospects both for the development of the social sciences and for the progress of historical study.

It is not every historian who has both the time and the opportunity for collaborative research, nor is it necessary that all historical research should be carried on in this fashion. As a matter of general policy, however, the Committee believes that the individual historian would be well advised to cultivate an awareness of what social scientists are doing, particularly in fields where the lines of inquiry and the types of data parallel his own. This is by no means inconsistent with the recommendation that he should also retain an attitude of qualified skepticism toward any *particular* methodological device which the other social sciences provide. These devices are not ends in themselves, but merely tools which are to be used if they facilitate historical research, discarded if they inhibit it. An uncritical acceptance as finally valid of any theory, hypothesis, or concept that has not been fully tested and found reliable is entirely unjustified and nothing in this report should be taken as sanctioning any such course.

It is not in the belief that historians will find it easy to make effective use of the techniques of the other social sciences that the Committee presents its findings and recommendations, but rather in the hope that a conscientious attempt to explore the possibilities and limitations of these other social science approaches may assist historians to form their own judgments as to their value and feasibility. The virtue of this exposition is not only that it suggests the possibilities of certain types of analysis, but also that it makes necessary a critical re-examination of the fundamental problem of the nature of history as a branch of intellectual activity. Training in thought about history seems to this Committee, as to its predecessor, as important as training in any particular type of analysis. The Committee, in its consultations with experts from other fields, found no basis whatsoever for the fancy that some magic formula or method derived from another discipline would enable the historians to produce "scientific" results. The value of the use of social science in history is to be judged entirely by the fruitfulness of its results when applied intelligently to suitable material. The purpose of this report is not to make out a case for its uncritical adoption, but to suggest what intelligent application means.

3   A SURVEY OF CONCEPTS AND VIEWPOINTS IN THE SOCIAL SCIENCES

The historian can gain a working knowledge of the social sciences only from wide reading, discussion, and application of specific concepts to historical materials.[1] In the course of such study the scholar will become familiar with social science points of view and with an analytical as distinct from a narrative approach to the past. To provide a start for historians who wish to explore these possibilities, we present a summary of areas of interest in the social sciences together with references to recent writing in each field.

Justification for this very brief survey rests upon the assumption that while precision in terminology and conceptualization is necessary within the disciplines for the building of theoretical models, it is less important in the initial approach to practical problems of research. It is our belief that the scholar from another field needs primarily a general idea of the methods and interests of a particular discipline. A little knowledge may be a dangerous thing, but it is a necessary risk for the general historian. On the basis of a limited understanding and

[1] The historian seeking to become informed on ideas and methods currently developing among other social scientists can well begin by consulting colleagues or other specialists in particular fields, who can be helpful in guiding the historian to critical reviews and appraisals published from time to time. The following may be cited, merely as illustrations: M. Brewster Smith, "Some Recent Texts in Social Psychology," *Psychological Bulletin,* 50:150–159 (March 1953); Arthur H. Cole, "Committee on Research in Economic History," *Journal of Economic History,* 13: 79–87 (Winter 1953); Samuel A. Stouffer, "Measurement in Sociology," *American Sociological Review,* 18:591–597 (December 1953); Social Science Research Council Interuniversity Summer Research Seminar on Political Behavior Research, "Research in Political Behavior," *American Political Science Review,* 46:1003–1045 (December 1952); Roy Macridis and Richard Cox, "Research in Comparative Politics," *American Political Science Review,* 47:641–675 (September 1953). Also, more extensive surveys occasionally become available and convenient, for example: A. L. Kroeber and others, *Anthropology Today* (Chicago: University of Chicago Press, 1953); *A Survey of Contemporary Economics,* Vol. I, Howard S. Ellis, ed. (Philadelphia: American Economic Association, 1948), and Vol. II, Bernard F. Haley, ed. (Homewood, Ill.: American Economic Association, 1952). These will be referred to at appropriate points in this chapter.

some acquaintance with bibliography, the scholar faced with a research problem can acquire the appropriate special knowledge. The weakness of historical research from this standpoint has not been so much mis-application of social science concepts as neglect of important areas of interest.

In the present stage of social science knowledge, with many common problems of method and terminology still unresolved, a survey of the field involves much subjective evaluation of the promise of various areas of advance. The following selection, therefore, represents in general the opinion of the writer, and less directly that of the Committee and its advisers, as to what may be of most value to other historians. The discussion is intended to be suggestive. In actual research each scholar must explicitly define, or redefine for his own purposes, the concepts, terms, and modes of analysis derived from other fields. We hope, how-ever, that the chapter will suggest to readers unfamiliar with the social sciences fruitful ways of thinking about and classifying the phenomena and processes of change that they encounter in historical study.

ANTHROPOLOGY

Anthropology is perhaps the social science most congenial to his-torians. Anthropologists and historians face many common problems, and in discussing them show similar divisions of opinion. The border between archaeology and history is indistinct; anthropologists tra-ditionally have studied the culture of primitive man, historians study civilized man, but again there is no sharp dividing line. We are fortu-nate in having an unusually up-to-date record of the best contemporary thought in anthropology. In the spring of 1952 the Wenner-Gren Foundation for Anthropological Research assembled an International Symposium which included most of the leading anthropologists; the papers prepared for the meetings have been published in *Anthro-pology Today*.[2] In addition, the discussions at the meetings were edited and published as *An Appraisal of Anthropology Today*.[3] The historian should certainly use these volumes as a starting point.

A major cause of confusion as to the place of anthropology in a scientific-humanistic classification is, just as in the case of history,

[2] A. L. Kroeber and others, *op. cit.* The volume contains carefully selected bibliographies.

[3] Sol Tax, Loren C. Eiseley, Irving Rouse, and Carl F. Voegelin, eds. (Chicago: University of Chicago Press, 1953).

the universality of its subject matter. This has led William L. Straus,. Jr. to say, "I do not think anthropology exists as a distinct entity as physics does. It exists merely as a meeting ground of people interested in man." [4] Robert Redfield's paper, "Relations of Anthropology to the Social Sciences and to the Humanities," in the Symposium, illustrates a tendency to talk of physical anthropology as a biological science, and cultural anthropology as a humanity without stressing its place among the social sciences. Redfield writes that "the human is more easily treated by the method of descriptive integration [the conventional method of historians] than by that of generalizing science." He further believes that in anthropology, "The literature does not show competent general propositions applicable to all cases within precisely defined classes and allowing of exact predictive application." [5]

In practice four distinct branches of anthropology have arisen: physical anthropology studies the biological evolution and racial differentiation of man; archaeology seeks to discover the character of man's prehistoric cultures; anthropological linguistics analyzes verbal and written culture; and cultural anthropology deals with current cultures, personality types, and human relations. Physical anthropology, in particular, has a set of highly specialized problems that have only an indirect bearing on the concerns of cultural anthropology.

In tracing the course of human evolution, the dispersal of mankind over the face of the earth, and the development of human cultures, anthropology necessarily deals with historical problems.[6] The methods of archaeology and physical anthropology are essentially those of history, with modifications appropriate to the data. The phase of physical anthropology, for example, that is concerned with human and primate evolution is substantially historical inquiry. Within cultural anthropology it is increasingly customary to distinguish culture history or ethnology from social anthropology. The former deals with the history of diffusion, migrations, and culture change; the latter concentrates

---

[4] *Ibid.*, p. 153.

[5] Kroeber and others, *Anthropology Today*, pp. 732, 735.

[6] Except as noted, the following pages are based on the Committee's discussions with Clyde Kluckhohn and A. L. Kroeber, of whom the former submitted a written memorandum from which we have quoted without formal citation, and on later discussion with A. Irving Hallowell. For a popularized account of the field see Kluckhohn, *Mirror for Man: The Relation of Anthropology to Modern Life* (New York: Whittlesey House, 1949).

upon the study of specific types of culture, personality, and social structure.[7]

All aspects of historical anthropology try to trace the genetic linkages in a chronological series of related phenomena. Could the fossil gibbons found in Egypt be ancestral to human beings or only to modern gibbons? Has the Neanderthal species of the Europe and Palestine of 20,000 years ago left no descendants, or is modern man the result of a cross between the Neanderthal and Cro-Magnon types?

Culture, as one of the major concepts and research areas of anthropology, must be discussed in some detail. Viewed at one level it includes the composite of the capabilities and habits learned by man as a member of society. But behavior is not generally regarded as culture. Rather, concrete behavior or habits are part of the raw data from which the anthropologist infers and abstracts culture.[8] The physical results of past behavior such as chairs, automobiles or other goods, called artifacts, comprise the other class of raw data. Culture, thus, is not something that is seen but an inferential construct. This worries a few anthropological positivists a great deal, but one can point to excellent precedents in the physical sciences. No one has ever seen an electromagnetic field. This is also an inferential construct but, like culture, a highly useful one in helping us to understand phenomena and to predict existences and events. The more homogeneous societies have *a* culture, often with regional or class variants. Some societies—or at any rate nations—possess more than one culture. Conversely, cultures—or at least subcultures—sometimes belong to communities or other segments of a society rather than to the society as a whole.

History is a sequence of particular cultures, provided the word "sequence" does not imply too much as to the inevitability of particular cultural forms following one another in a fixed order. Each

[7] See Glyn E. Daniel, *A Hundred Years of Archaeology* (London: G. Duckworth & Co., 1950).

[8] Anthropological theorists of culture are divided along lines corresponding to philosophical nominalism and realism. Some assert that culture is behavior, others that culture is always and inevitably an abstraction from behavior. The latter view, which helps in distinguishing purely physical traits from culture, is used in the following discussion. See Clyde Kluckhohn and William H. Kelly, "The Concept of Culture," in Ralph Linton, ed., *The Science of Man in the World Crisis* (New York: Columbia University Press, 1945); and Melville J. Herskovits, *Man and His Works: The Science of Cultural Anthropology* (New York: Alfred A. Knopf, 1948).

culture is the precipitate of its history. Cultures are not constants; they are always undergoing change.[9] A cultural fabric at any point of time may be compared to a shot silk of many varied colors. It is transparent, not opaque. To the trained eye, threads of the past gleam beneath the surface of the present. On the other hand, Ortega y Gasset's "Man has no nature; he has history" is an overstatement. While cultures are the products of history, history is influenced by man's biological nature and physical environment. In human affairs one can never start with a clean slate at any particular point in time. Although there is some disagreement on the point among anthropologists, it may be that the inherent potentialities of the human organism and the limits and demands of the generalized human situation are such that a roughly similar sequence of cultural types appears wherever the natural order of events is not disturbed by diffusion from centers of "higher" culture.

Careful observations of the words and deeds of human beings make it certain that many of their acts are not a consequence simply of physical and biological potentialities and limitations. If this were the case, the possible variations within a defined field of biological and physical forces would be random. But they definitely are not random. The variations within different human groups that have some historical continuity tend beyond all possible doubt to cluster around certain norms. These norms are demonstrably different between groups that have different historical continuities. These observed stylizations of action which are characteristic of human groups are the basis for isolating the cultural dimension of action.

Culture traits and culture patterns, defined as behavioral uniformities such as ways of dressing or conducting religious services, are first-order abstractions, arrived at mainly by induction from direct observation. But a great deal of experience indicates that important kinds of prediction are possible only if there is a systematic understanding of the organization of a culture at a "deeper" level. This implicit culture is a second-order abstraction, an inferential construct by the observer. It attempts to describe the habitual categories, the customary tacit premises or values—a whole sector of the culture of which the *culture carriers* are unaware or minimally aware in any systematic fashion. The unconscious assumptions characteristically made by individuals of the same class and environment constitute a

[9] On cultural change see A. L. Kroeber, *Anthropology* (New York: Harcourt, Brace and Company, 1948), Chapter 10.

set of thematic principles—of common denominators implicit in a wide range of cultural content. There tends to be a unifying philosophy, much of which remains implicit, behind the way of life of each society at any given point in its history. An example is the importance accorded to the individual and his happiness in Western European and American civilization. From the life ways of his cultural environment the ordinary individual derives most of his mental outlook; but he has little awareness of his culture or of its historic depth and diversity. Methods for arriving at and describing the implicit culture in a standard way are only just being developed, but on the part of anthropologists there is a rapidly growing recognition of their indispensable importance.[10]

Organized human life is always in some sense a balancing of opposed tendencies. In part the opposition consists of the contrast between actual behavior patterns in existing situations, on the one hand, and the expectancies defined by the sanctioned patterns of the culture.

Some aspects of a culture are carried by all (or virtually all) members of a cultural group. These are called "universals," as contrasted with "alternatives" and "specialities." Glorification of the mother is universal in American culture, whereas specific religious practices offer alternatives, and many different occupational patterns are specialities.

A culture area ordinarily coincides with certain other regionally limiting or defining factors. The life of a people is organized not only by its culture but by the challenges, opportunities, and limitations imposed by climate, topography, flora and fauna, other natural resources, and location in relation to other cultures.

Special environmental pressure or deviant individuals account for the shift of creative activity into new lines.[11] A reorganizing force seems to arise through the increase of variable behavior under strong stimulus. For example, an individual who in ordinary times would be punished as a deviant, or dismissed as an eccentric, may in extraordinary times become the founder of a powerful new religion. At such times people generally feel disturbed. They behave in trial and error fashion to get relief. Some special individual's phantasies or private rituals make emotional sense and are taken over and socialized

[10] See Margaret Mead, "National Character," in Kroeber and others, *Anthropology Today*, pp. 642–667.

[11] See H. G. Barnett, *Innovation: The Basis of Cultural Change* (New York: McGraw-Hill Book Company, 1953); and S. C. Gilfillan, *The Sociology of Invention* (Chicago: Follett Publishing Co., 1935).

by the group. There is evidence to suggest that, in general, the mal-adjusted and malintegrated individuals within a society are most receptive to innovation whether it originates from within or without.

Up to a point, an integrating principle or powerful configuration of the implicit culture will hold culture change along certain lines and indeed block all change beyond a certain limit. But, if the external pressures are strong enough, these factors of the implicit culture will finally give way, although they may also "come back" later. Not infrequently the visible aspects of a culture, in areas such as literature, dress, and technology, will alter markedly within a generation. But the sensitive student will report that although much of the old culture has gone, certain major themes or patterns remain the same. *Plus ça change, plus c'est la même chose.*[12]

Learning that is genuinely new in the sense that it involves a breakdown of pre-existent patterns seldom occurs except when external forces are very strong. Intolerance and repression (adverse sanctions) tend to be negative evidences of the emergence of a "new" culture. Anthropologists also speak of the absorption of new patterns destructive to an existing culture as antagonistic acculturation.

While concepts related to culture and culture change offer the greatest immediate contribution to the historian, two new areas of anthropology, personality structure and universal characteristics of human nature, offer great promise for the future. A. Irving Hallowell in an essay called "Culture, Personality, and Society," in the International Symposium, discusses the relation of these new fields to older anthropological interests.[13] He contends that "it is being more clearly recognized than heretofore that society, culture, and personality cannot be postulated as completely independent variables. . . . A human society, by minimal definition, requires organized relations, differentiated roles, and patterns of social interaction, not simply an aggregation of people." [14] The relations of personality structures or types to given cultures have still to be clarified, and the modern concept of personality will be discussed further in the section dealing with the field of social psychology.

One of the main effects of focusing attention on personality structure

[12] In the foregoing paragraphs adapted from the Kluckhohn memorandum, the historian may readily note the "humanistic" spirit in cultural anthropology.

[13] Kroeber and others, *Anthropology Today*, pp. 597–620. See especially the bibliography, pp. 616–620.

[14] *Ibid.*, pp. 600–601.

is to emphasize the processes by which the individual learns his culture. This study is drawing anthropologists and psychologists together and promises to develop new theories of perception that should ultimately be of use to the historian.

Redfield says of the other new emphasis in cultural anthropology: "The conception of universal human qualities has reappeared, among other places, in the recognition recently given by such men as Firth and Kluckhohn to the existence of moral values universal in all cultures." [15] According to Hallowell, "A human social order, for example, is always a moral order. . . . Self-awareness is as inherent in the human situation as are social structure and culture." [16] Since the universal occurrence of such practices as ceremonializing death has long been recognized by anthropologists, the new interest is in a closer and more sophisticated search for the uniform personality characteristics behind such universal drives and ceremonies.

SOCIOLOGY

Like anthropology, sociology is an all-embracing study of human actions and relations. The sociologist defines his field as the study of society, its structure, functions, and processes.[17] If one looks at the boundaries implied in such a definition there appears to be little difference between the areas of cultural or social anthropology and sociology; there are, however, differences in the foci of interest and in methods of approach. One aspect of the difference is illustrated in Kingsley Davis' discussion of "social versus cultural change." "By 'social change' is meant only such alterations as occur in social organization—that is, the structure and functions of society. Social change thus forms only a part of what is essentially a broader category called 'cultural change.' . . . Since our interest is focused on the narrowed topic [social change] we shall not become involved in such matters as the evolution of phonetic sounds, the history of art forms, the transition of musical styles, or the development of mathematical theory. Of course, no part of culture is totally unrelated to the social order,

[15] *Ibid.*, p. 730.

[16] *Ibid.*, pp. 614–615.

[17] Except as noted, the following discussion is based on a memorandum submitted in 1948 by Harry Alpert, and his discussion of it with the Committee on Historiography. The present draft has been carefully read by Leonard S. Cottrell, Jr. and Donald Young and revised in accordance with their suggestions. See Georges Gurvitch and Wilbert E. Moore, eds., *Twentieth Century Sociology* (New York: Philosophical Library, 1945) for a symposium on the then current state of sociological knowledge.

but it remains true that changes may occur in these branches without noticeably affecting the social system. Sociologically, therefore, we are interested in cultural change only to the extent that it arises from or has an effect on social organization." [18]

In studying social interaction from this point of view, however, the sociologist sometimes obscures the distinction between social and cultural processes. This has a tendency to minimize the importance of historical continuity, generally seen in the content of communication (cultural), and to stress the importance of change in the methods of communication (social). The use of the terms cultural and social also illustrates the difficulty in setting boundaries between the various all-inclusive social sciences. To say that sociology is concerned with the structure and functioning of society, and anthropology with the content and patterns of culture establishes a line that neither discipline will in fact recognize.

Historical research has been largely concerned with social change, and thus spans the field of sociology seen in time perspective. But the limitations of historical source material and the pursuit of special threads of social change, such as political, military, or religious, have diverted the attention of historians from the general sociological frameworks of past societies. Most sociologists, on the other hand, have been chiefly interested in studying the patterns or norms of contemporary social interaction in their own societies.

It would be a mistake, however, to assume that sociologists have worked out any generally accepted model of the structure and interaction of society. In the words of Robert K. Merton, "the growing contributions of sociological theory to its sister-disciplines lie more in the realm of general sociological orientations than in that of specific confirmed hypotheses. . . . Despite the many volumes dealing with the history of sociological theory and despite the plethora of empirical investigations, sociologists (including the writer) may discuss the logical criteria of sociological laws without citing a single instance which fully satisfies these criteria." [19] Earlier in the same volume Merton writes: "one must admit that a large part of what is now called sociological theory consists of *general orientations toward data,*

18 Kingsley Davis, *Human Society* (New York: Macmillan Company, 1949), pp. 622–623. By permission.

19 Robert K. Merton, *Social Theory and Social Structure: Toward the Codification of Theory and Research* (Glencoe, Ill.: Free Press, 1949), pp. 86, 92. The first three chapters of this book are an excellent introduction to social research.

suggesting types of variables which need somehow to be taken into account, rather than clear, verifiable statements of relationships between specified variables." [20] The following discussion of sociology, therefore, takes the form of general descriptions of some of the concepts used in the various areas of interest. This procedure is, of course, unsatisfactory from a theoretical point of view, but appears to be reasonable in the circumstances.

The study of values, an increasing interest among sociologists, coincides closely with the work of many cultural anthropologists on cultural patterns and themes. In writing on this subject members of the two disciplines continually refer to each other's work.

Robin Williams, sociologist, defines value "as any aspect of a situation, event, or object that is invested with a *preferential interest* as being 'good,' 'bad,' 'desirable,' and the like." [21] Recognizing the circularity of a definition that simply substitutes "preferential interest" for "value," he goes on to a description of the boundaries and qualities of values. Values are described as abstract concepts drawn from the individual's experience; they are emotionally (or affectively) charged; they provide the criteria by which goals are chosen; and they are important in determining behavior.

Kluckhohn, as an anthropologist, sees behind the overtly expressed values (such as belief in physical science) the implicit system of cultural themes, while Williams says: "To speak of value systems is, then, to imply that values are not simply distributed at random, but are instead interdependent, arranged in a pattern, and subject to reciprocal . . . variation." [22]

Turning to the question of the "ideal types" of value orientation in America, both writers find much the same basic patterns or themes. Kluckhohn lists: faith in the rational, a need for moralistic rationalization, an optimistic conviction that rational effort counts, romantic individualism and the cult of the common man, high valuation of change (which is ordinarily taken to mean progress), the conscious quest of pleasure.[23] Williams' fundamental group consists of: active

[20] *Ibid.*, p. 9; for an attempt at a comprehensive plan for studying social phenomena see Talcott Parsons, *The Social System* (Glencoe, Ill.: Free Press, 1951).

[21] Robin M. Williams, Jr., *American Society: A Sociological Interpretation* (New York: Alfred A. Knopf, 1951), p. 374; for a general discussion see pp. 372–442, and also Ralph K. White, *Value-Analysis: The Nature and Use of the Method* (New York: Society for the Psychological Study of Social Issues, 1951).

[22] Williams, *op. cit.*, p. 385.

[23] Kluckhohn, *Mirror for Man,* p. 232.

mastery as opposed to passive acceptance, interest in the external world of things, emphasis on change, faith in rationalism, an emphasis on orderliness, belief in equality rather than superordinate-subordinate relationships, emphasis on the individual personality.[24]

Relatively little social science research has been carried on to document specific values with substantial evidence, or to develop hypotheses about their interrelations and operation in controlling behavior. But some social scientists regard this as one of the most important areas for future work. Kluckhohn writes: "The greatest advance in contemporary anthropological theory is probably the increasing recognition that there is something more to culture than artifacts, linguistic texts, and lists of atomized traits."[25] Historians, implicitly at least, have always subscribed to this view, but they have seldom tried to systematize or classify their observations of values in the written records of earlier culture.

Group analysis is currently one of the areas of research in which sociologists are most active. Social groups are seen as persons regularly in contact or communication who for certain purposes identify themselves with each other. Small intimate groups may range from a family to the members of a club or a neighborhood. To distinguish such groups from larger and less closely associated aggregates such as a theater audience, some sociologists use the terms primary and secondary, but disagree somewhat as to the distinguishing characteristics. Other sociologists have developed the concept of quasi group to cover social classes, publics, and other aggregates or portions of the community that have no recognizable structure, but whose members have certain interests or modes of behavior in common which may at any time lead them to form themselves into definite groups. The nature and type of social groups, the bases of group formation, the processes of group cohesion, the conditions of group action, and the structure and patterns of intergroup relations are among the major problems with which this area of sociology is concerned.[26]

Agreement has not been reached on any rigid distinction between groups and associations. Any aggregate may be considered a group if it has a common goal and some degree of cohesiveness. These

24 Williams, op. cit., pp. 441–442.

25 Kluckhohn, "The Study of Culture," in Daniel Lerner, Harold D. Lasswell, and others, eds., The Policy Sciences: Recent Developments in Scope and Method (Stanford: Stanford University Press, 1951), p. 89.

26 See Kingsley Davis, Human Society, pp. 289–307.

factors appear to be more important than the size of the aggregate in determining group behavior. Similarly, in dealing with small groups, emphasis is put on intimacy and duration of relations as well as on whether and how frequently the members meet and have direct personal contacts.

Some suggestive ideas have been developed in analysis of group behavior, from consideration of the way in which members of the same group regard each other as against all outsiders. This in-group versus out-group distinction has supplied clues to the understanding of intergroup relations. The concepts refer to the fact, well known to historians, that group relations affect ethical judgments and ways of thinking. What is an excusable error by a member of one's own political party, for instance, is a gross betrayal of trust in a member of the opposition. An extreme form of group attitude is represented by the view of things in which one's own group is the center of everything and all others are scaled with reference to it. But this phenomenon, called ethnocentrism, is only one aspect of the process by which members of groups develop conceptions of themselves and of others. Group images, that is, the typical mental pictures that the members have of themselves and others and that serve as basic frames of reference in terms of which they define their relations to one another, play an important part in determining the nature of intergroup contacts. Social groups are also seen as "sifting devices" whereby people in a large urban population are organized in associations having recognized positions of prestige or power, such as churches, exclusive clubs, or boards of directors.[27]

Recent research on industrial morale, clique behavior, voting behavior, and group dynamics has tended to reaffirm the sociological concept of the influential character of the small, direct, face-to-face group, and has increased understanding of the nature of interpersonal relations in the small group. For example, in *The People's Choice* Lazarsfeld, Berelson, and Gaudet stress the role of personal relationships and face-to-face contacts in determining how one votes in a presidential election.[28]

[27] See W. Lloyd Warner and Paul S. Lunt, *The Social Life of a Modern Community*, Yankee City Series, Vol. I (New Haven: Yale University Press, 1941), pp. 301–355.

[28] Paul F. Lazarsfeld, Bernard Berelson, and Hazel Gaudet, *The People's Choice: How the Voter Makes Up His Mind in a Presidential Campaign* (2nd ed.; New York: Columbia University Press, 1948).

Groups can grow so large that a great many people of a country feel themselves part of the in-group, as was perhaps the case in the early stages of the French Revolution. But, as indicated in the American election study just cited, groups form within groups. In times of crisis there is a tendency toward a defensive heightening of in-group feeling and permanence of group relationships. In war and revolution, for example, there is assumed to be a shift in the relative importance of different types of groups. Basic natural groups such as family or neighborhood groups become weakened in favor of larger political groups which in normal times have less importance in society. Such changes in turn alter the character of social institutions.

The most important primary group in Western society is the family, but there are few sociological concepts regarding its character and dynamics that go beyond historical description. One reason for this is that much research in this field has been oriented to what have been regarded as problems of the family, such as divorce, desertion, or illegitimacy, rather than to family processes and structure. Another reason appears to be that it is hard to separate the social interactions of the family from biological and psychological factors, and the latter fall largely outside the conventional field of sociology. Conversely psychologists study the family from the standpoint of parent-child relationships without much regard for social or cultural pressures and relations. Historians, however, may gain new ideas and perceptions by studying the literature on the family by anthropologists, social psychologists, and sociologists.[29]

While action by individuals is often eccentric and impossible to forecast, each society has a set of normal expectations or ideals as to how people should act. These social norms, the way people should

---

[29] The May 1948 issue of the *American Journal of Sociology*, 53:417–495, is entirely devoted to articles on the American family. The only detailed historical accounts of American families are Arthur W. Calhoun, *A Social History of the American Family from Colonial Times to the Present* (3 vols., Cleveland: Arthur H. Clark Company, 1917–19; 1 vol., New York: Barnes & Noble, 1945); and John Sirjamaki, *The American Family in the Twentieth Century* (Cambridge: Harvard University Press, 1953). Leonard S. Cottrell, Jr., "The Present Status and Future Orientation of Research on the Family," *American Sociological Review*, 13:123–136 (April 1948), offers the historian a brief introduction to the field. See also E. Franklin Frazier, *The Negro Family in the United States* (Chicago: University of Chicago Press, 1939); Willystine Goodsell, *A History of Marriage and the Family* (rev. ed.; New York: Macmillan Company, 1934); and Willard Waller, *The Family: A Dynamic Interpretation* (New York: Cordon Company, 1938; rev. by Reuben Hill, New York: Dryden Press, 1951).

behave, are in turn types of culture patterns. Since William Graham Sumner's time they have been divided into folkways, traditional standardized practices that are not obligatory upon the individual, and mores, patterns regarded as essential for social welfare and enforced by strong social pressures. Such pressures for conformity, called sanctions, may range from internal religious or conscientious urges to laws or physical force.[30]

The sociologist further describes the normative structure of society in terms already used by historians. Institutions, customs, morality, religion, conventions, etiquette, fashions, status, office, and prestige all have a familiar ring. For purposes of theorizing these terms may be given more precise meanings than is thought necessary in most historical research.

The word "institution" may serve to illustrate some of the semantic problems raised by the quest for more exact definitions. This term has been used by all the social sciences, and considerable discrepancies between different usages have developed. In general, it refers to either an organized system of actions, or a system of rules or norms of behavior accepted and recognized by individuals in a group.[31] To sociologists who deal with temporal processes, however, the concept seems also to include the idea of persistence or structural stability through time. For the historian, therefore, the most useful conception of an institution would appear to be that of an organized system of actions that exhibits an appreciable degree of temporal continuity, such as the family, the church, or the state. As the examples suggest, this conception is by no means inconsistent with an awareness of the normative, or behavior-controlling, aspect. The functional approach to institutions focuses on the roles that institutions play or are believed to play in satisfying human needs.

Among the numerous ideas that have developed from institutional analysis, the following five are of special interest to the historian: (1) the persistence of certain basic institutions such as the family or religious ceremonies as universal features of social organization; (2) the transference and shifting of functions over time from one institution to another; (3) the interdependence of institutions so that changes in one create changes in others; (4) the operation of a principle of congeniality or a "strain towards consistency" among institutions in a

30 For a good general discussion see Davis, *op. cit.*, pp. 52–119.

31 The anthropologist sees these social phenomena as culture patterns and seldom employs the word "institution."

given society; (5) the operation of a principle of institutional inertia, or the tendency of institutions to persist through organization for self-perpetuation.

Anthropological and sociological research have both called particular attention to the importance of status even in democratic societies. They see any given status as part of a system of social stratification by which the members of a society rank each other in terms of prestige, and other types of social rewards. Social classes may be defined as aggregates of individuals, often without specific inherent differentiating characteristics, who enter into and maintain relations with one another on a basis of equality, in contrast to other members of the community from whom they are distinguished (for the moment at least) by socially recognized standards of inferiority and superiority. In some but not all societies, and particularly in the United States, the principal basis for the formation of social classes is an economic one, the standards of inferiority and superiority being earning and spending potentials. Members of a given class characteristically develop a similar mode of life and similar attitudes and patterns of behavior and, with varying degrees of explicitness, a sense of belonging together. The sociologist is concerned with the bases of class differentiation (that is, the criteria that determine the class positions of individuals), with the analysis of the patterns of behavior characteristic of different classes, and with the types of stress that arise between classes.[32] All these matters are, needless to say, of prime importance to the historian.

The movement of persons from class to class in the social hierarchy is called social mobility. When because of differentiating characteristics that can be acquired only by birth, such as Hindu religious status or brown skin, the amount of vertical mobility approaches zero, the class structure may be called a caste system. On the other hand, if there is a large degree of vertical mobility, as for white persons in the United States, that part of the society is said to have an open-class system. One does not need to accept a Marxian interpretation to recognize the extent to which historical change depends on the caste and class structure in a given society, and the frequency of movement in an upward or downward direction. Historians may be particularly interested in such questions as: who moves up and who moves down? Do such move-

---

[32] See, for example, Merton, *Social Theory and Social Structure*, pp. 115–199; and Reinhard Bendix and Seymour M. Lipset, eds., *Class, Status and Power* (Glencoe, Ill.: Free Press, 1953).

ments take place within relatively small ranges of the social scale, or do they involve relatively long-range movements, as from the lowest to the very highest class stratum? For example, did American business and political leaders at various periods rise from poor farms or city slums or did they generally have prosperous middle-class parents? [33] In addition to studying the extent, direction, and nature of the movement of individuals up and down the social scale, it is necessary to inquire into the channels of mobility. What are the characteristic career patterns in society? To what extent do church, school, army, political parties, and other institutional groups serve as "elevators" through which individuals move up and down?

In a stratified social situation those at the top level with respect to power and influence may be called the elite regardless of desirable or undesirable qualities or the efficiency with which they play their roles. Analyses of elites have included studies of their composition, their personality characteristics, their methods of maintaining power, their basic thought patterns, and their "circulation," or permanency.[34]

Taking the view, congenial to historians, of seeing society as a background for the actions of individuals, social scientists have developed some useful organizing concepts. An individual performing any given function or series of functions, such as being a father or fulfilling the duties of governor of a state, is regarded as playing that particular role. The way the person acts is his individual interpretation of the role, but social norms create expectations in the minds of other interested people as to how the role should be played. These reflections of the norms as conceived by a certain group are its conception of the social role for performing that particular function. In other words, a social role is an understanding shared more or less fully by the members of a group as to what a given position entails for any indi-

[33] See, for example, Frances W. Gregory and Irene D. Neu, "The American Industrial Elite in the 1870's," and William Miller, "The Business Elite in Business Bureaucracies," in William Miller, ed., *Men in Business* (Cambridge: Harvard University Press, 1952), pp. 193–211, 286–305; William Miller, "American Historians and the Business Elite," *Journal of Economic History*, 9:184–208 (May 1949); C. Wright Mills, *White Collar: The American Middle Classes* (New York: Oxford University Press, 1951), and "The American Business Elite: A Collective Portrait," *Journal of Economic History*, 5(suppl.):20–44 (December 1945).

[34] See, for example, Thomas C. Cochran, *Railroad Leaders, 1845–1890: The Business Mind in Action* (Cambridge: Harvard University Press, 1953); and Alvin W. Gouldner, ed., *Studies in Leadership* (New York: Harper & Brothers, 1950).

viduals who occupy it. It is a group idea of how certain social functions should be performed.[35]

While this seems clear, it is necessary to point out the existence of considerable differences and ambiguities in the ways in which the terms "role" and "function" are used by different writers.[36] In general, "function" refers to the dynamic aspects of a role—the behavior expected of any individual occupying that role. For example, the role of "butcher" is really defined in terms of what a butcher does; if a butcher does not cut meat, he ceases to be a butcher. The existence of group ideas as to how the functions associated with a certain social role should be performed, however, does not necessarily imply that these functions will actually be performed in the most efficient way, or indeed at all. The expectations may be traditional beliefs that no longer fit the physical realities of the situation. Indeed, the performance of the role in the prescribed manner may actually thwart the attainment of the end manifestly sought. In this case the role may be called "dysfunctional." But roles dysfunctional on the physical level, such as the king of a poor nation performing an elaborate and expensive royal ceremony, may still be functional in other respects.

Use of the concepts of role and function provides a way of analyzing individual behavior and motivation in complex social situations. These concepts suggest that the historian should try to extend his investigation of the performance of a social function to the various roles played by the individuals who perform it. Where such analyses have been made there has usually been a difference in emphasis by sociologists and historians. The sociologist sees the individual roles as material for identifying analytical norms and patterns; the historian is more likely to be concerned with the deviant roles that induce change than with an understanding of the pattern of the normal ones. Deviant roles, however, cannot be adequately understood without an understanding of the norms from which deviation takes place.

Social roles vary greatly in their scope or definition, depending ultimately on the homogeneity and force of the expectations held by the

[35] See Leland H. Jenks, "The Role Structure of Entrepreneurial Personality," in Harvard University Research Center in Entrepreneurial History, *Change and the Entrepreneur: Postulates and Patterns for Entrepreneurial History* (Cambridge: Harvard University Press, 1949), pp. 133–152; and Gardner Murphy, *Personality: A Biosocial Approach to Origins and Structure* (New York: Harper & Brothers, 1947), pp. 784–795.

[36] See Lionel J. Neiman and J. W. Hughes, "The Problem of the Concept of Role," *Social Forces*, 30:141–149 (December 1951).

group which prescribes the particular role. These, in turn, depend on the size of the group and the importance that it ascribes to the function and the importance of the sanctions of this group to the player of the role.[37] A corporation president plays a role principally set by the expectations of his fellow officers and directors. In relation to business matters, at least, this is likely to be a closely defined role, because the prescribing group is a small face-to-face one, and the actions of the president are of great importance to them.[38] In such a case any conduct that appears to endanger performance of the function, even such matters as a disorganized private life, may be adversely sanctioned in forceful ways. Therefore, it is possible to establish a number of norms, or to define a social role that will be reliably adhered to by the executive of the large corporation in the performance of his job.

Another way of viewing the same social control over role playing is to see each player as having a number of groups, called reference groups, whose expectations he would like to fulfill but whose sanctioning force varies.[39] Presumably the actor will have to satisfy the expectations of those groups that have the power of censorship if he wants to continue playing the role, while other groups may be disappointed without being able to exert any immediate pressure. In the days before popular election, a United States senator's relations with his political party machine and with the voting public in his state would represent these differing types of social control.

While values, groups, norms, institutions, social structure, and roles are of interest to all sociologists, there are other areas of study that constitute special subfields. Urban or rural sociology, communications, race relations, criminology, and population are among the more important specialties.

Study of the transition in advanced industrial nations from rural to urban folkways and mores offers an excellent opportunity for cooperation between historians and sociologists. Much serious historical

[37] See Robert K. Merton and Paul F. Lazarsfeld, eds., *Continuities in Social Research: Studies in the Scope and Method of "The American Soldier"* (Glencoe, Ill.: Free Press, 1950).

[38] See Cochran, *Railroad Leaders,* Chapter 16, for an attempt to establish historically the norms of a social role.

[39] For further discussion of roles and sanctions see Samuel A. Stouffer and others, *The American Soldier: Adjustment During Army Life,* Studies in Social Psychology in World War II, Vol. I (Princeton: Princeton University Press, 1949), pp. 112–118.

research and much historical fiction have dealt with changing rural
culture, but have not been phrased or synthesized in ways satisfactory
to sociologists. Family relations, childhood conditioning, social roles,
and socialization in general are affected by the shift from rural to
urban living, and under modern conditions of communication the
change is reflected in the rural as well as the urban areas. This is so
much the case that some sociologists think that almost all of the
United States is essentially urban in culture.[40]

City life is apt to be regarded as less "natural" to the human organism because it is more impersonal in its contacts, more vicarious
in its participations, and less secure than rural life. Each of these
assumptions is open to question or modification, but together they
are held to be a cause of social disorganization in cities.

Social disorganization may be defined as a decrease in the influence
of existing social rules of behavior upon individual members of a
group.[41] The decrease may be of differing degree, ranging from a
single infraction of some particular rule by one individual up to
general decay of all institutions of the group. Closely related to this
view of social disorganization is the concept of *anomie* or normless-
ness, the condition often found among the lower classes of great cities
where the social norms and sanctions that formerly, in smaller communities, gave direction to an individual's conduct are rendered mean-
ingless and impotent.[42] The concept of anomie is frequently used in
analyses of urban industrial civilization and in social studies of the
factory system.

Some sociologists have given the name human ecology to the study

[40] See Paul K. Hatt and Albert J. Reiss, Jr., eds., *Reader in Urban Sociology*
(Glencoe, Ill.: Free Press, 1951); Svend Riemer, *The Modern City* (New York:
Prentice-Hall, 1952); Louis Wirth, "Urbanism as a Way of Life," *American Journal
of Sociology*, 44:1–24 (July 1938).

[41] William I. Thomas and Florian Znaniecki, *The Polish Peasant in Europe and
America* (New York: Alfred A. Knopf, 1927), Vol. II, p. 1128; or see Edmund H.
Volkart, ed., *Social Behavior and Personality: Contributions of W. I. Thomas to
Theory and Social Research* (New York: Social Science Research Council, 1951),
p. 11.

[42] The term anomie was first used in this sense by Émile Durkheim. See his
works, *The Division of Labor in Society* (trans. George Simpson; Glencoe, Ill.:
Free Press, 1947), and *Suicide: A Study in Sociology* (trans. John A. Spaulding and
George Simpson; Glencoe, Ill.: Free Press, 1951). For later use of this concept see
Elton Mayo, *The Human Problems of an Industrial Civilization* (New York:
Macmillan Company, 1933), and Merton, *Social Theory and Social Structure*, pp.
125–150.

of the relations between man and his environment.[43] But they differ from other schools in limiting "environment" to material conditions. They see a city, for example, as the arena of competition for the use of valuable land, and of other forms of competition between adjacent groups. This has led to an emphasis on dividing the city into distinct socioeconomic areas, and to hypotheses, such as the concentric circle pattern, regarding growth.

The current interest in communication and learning processes is closely connected with the nature of urban industrial society. Mass exposure to radio, television, and journalism, and the rise of commercial polls have focused attention on how people acquire their opinions. Borrowing the term from Europe, some scholars call this field the sociology of knowledge.[44]

The fundamental proposition of this approach is that the processes involved in the construction of systems of thought that are believed to be true are socially and culturally conditioned. It follows from this that belief in any particular system of thought must be explicable in terms of certain characteristics of its social context. Such analysis challenges the historian to expand the conventional area of intellectual history to studies of the relation of class, occupational, and other social positions to the creation of or belief in certain systems of thought, and to other characteristics of the societies in which such beliefs are found. The dominant forms of thought in specific periods in a given society will presumably be favorable to some of the major goals or needs of that society, although this may not be explicitly recognized by the participants.

The term ideology is used in several ways, but commonly refers to any system of ideas that is consciously or unconsciously developed by a group in furthering its own interests, whether with respect to creating change or preserving the existing situation. On this basis, all shared patterns of belief and thought advanced for a social purpose, whether religious beliefs or political or economic doctrines, are ideologies.[45]

The assumption that certain types of knowledge can exist inde-

[43] See James A. Quinn, *Human Ecology* (New York: Prentice-Hall, 1950), p. 3.

[44] See, for example, Karl Mannheim, *Essays on the Sociology of Knowledge* (New York: Oxford University Press, 1952); and Merton, *Social Theory and Social Structure*, pp. 199–264.

[45] Stemming from the Marxist tradition, the term ideology is used (for example by Karl Mannheim) in contrast with "utopia" to refer to a system of ideas by which a class attempts to maintain its own status, while "utopia" refers to a system of ideas intended to foster change.

pendent of ideology is essential to the existence of science. Used in this sense, knowledge refers to the possession of ideas, ways of doing things, and other forms of communicable information, regardless of whether they are used to further the interests of particular social groups. There are many instances, of course, in which it is difficult to distinguish knowledge from ideology, and there are those who (though with doubtful logic) deny the distinction entirely. For the scholar who reads the writings of St. Thomas Aquinas (which as originally expounded argued a Catholic point of view and were therefore ideology) merely to add to his professional competence, the philosophy constitutes knowledge. On the other hand, for the scholar who employs Thomism to justify the interests of his particular group, the philosophy is ideology.

The problem of analyzing ideology or propaganda has led to the development of content analysis, which is defined by Bernard Berelson as "a research technique for the objective, systematic, and quantitative description of the manifest content of communication." [46] The frequency of occurrence of certain phrases, concepts, ideas, or verbal symbols is noted. This new way of analyzing rhetorical material is considerably more systematic than anything previously available. Its potential value has been illustrated in the analysis of German radio propaganda by Kris and Speier.[47] Obviously, this technique is of major interest to historians, but as in so much social research the initial problem is to decide on the categories to be investigated and the indices of their occurrence.

Paul Lazarsfeld, who has devoted himself particularly to measurement applied to discursive material, writes: "there is a direct line of logical continuity from qualitative classification [regularly used by historians for purposes of generalization] to the most rigorous forms of measurement, by way of intermediate devices of systematic ratings, ranking scales, multidimensional classifications, typologies, and simple quantitative indices. . . . One way to develop social science measurement is to *systematize these commonly performed research proce-*

[46] Bernard Berelson, *Content Analysis in Communication Research* (Glencoe, Ill.: Free Press, 1952), p. 18.

[47] Ernst Kris and Hans Speier, *German Radio Propaganda: Report on Home Broadcasts during the War* (New York: Oxford University Press, 1944). See also Bernard Berelson and Morris Janowitz, eds., *Reader in Public Opinion and Communication* (Glencoe, Ill.: Free Press, 1950); and W. Hayes Yeager and William E. Utterback, eds., "Communication and Social Action," *Annals of the American Academy of Political and Social Science*, Vol. 250 (March 1947).

dures, by codifying exactly what successful researchers do in carrying out these simpler forms of measurement and exploring their logical implications." [48]

Lazarsfeld's systematization will no doubt seem excessively elementary to historians used to proceeding by the more fluid intuitive rules of "descriptive integration." But such complete explicitness is necessary, and it often has unsuspected values. "It is certainly possible to make human judgment *somewhat* objective," according to Lazarsfeld, "by systematizing the training and instruction of classifiers as much as possible. As a rule, *any* degree of segmentation and specification of indicators makes classification more objective—more likely to be agreed upon and more easily communicable." [49]

An illustration of the value of advance segmentation and specification can be taken from the field of intellectual history. A hundred thousand letters written by men in roughly similar circumstances were to be examined by two or more readers. Unless a particular item of information was decided on in advance as one of the categories to be looked for, no reader on the basis of his memory or the thoroughness of his notes could reliably affirm or deny that the item had appeared in one of the letters. By checking for negations as well as affirmations of certain anticipated characteristics it was possible to establish a considerable number of uniformities in ideas and attitudes that could then be put together as evidence for the existence of a coherent social role, capable of explaining and even forecasting behavior.[50]

The study of communication will advance as the process of learning is better understood. But research on this latter subject falls largely in the field of psychology and will be discussed presently.

The field of race relations, involving primarily the study of minorities distinguished by color or alien cultural characteristics such as language, was stimulated in American sociology by the heavy immigration of the early twentieth century and the enduring problem of the Negro.[51] Since the end of mass immigration and the gradual

[48] "Qualitative Measurement in the Social Sciences: Classification, Typologies, and Indices," with Allen H. Barton, in Lerner, Lasswell, and others, eds., *The Policy Sciences,* p. 155.

[49] *Ibid.,* p. 166.

[50] See Cochran, *Railroad Leaders,* Chapter 1.

[51] For a good summary of the earlier writing see Donald R. Young, *American Minority Peoples: A Study in Racial and Cultural Conflicts in the United States* (New York: Harper & Brothers, 1932). See also William I. Thomas and Florian

acculturation of the earlier migrants attention has focused increasingly on the latter problem.[52] Sociological study of race relations has been descriptive, and empirical rather than theoretical. In this field there appear to be few concepts or hypotheses with which historians are not already familiar.

Criminologists, who see crime as largely a problem of cultural maladjustment, deal with much the same material as students of minority problems.[53] Except for brief discussions under some heading such as social disorganization, textbooks usually treat criminology as a specialty lying outside the central field of sociology.[54]

DEMOGRAPHY

Population study may be regarded as a special area of sociology, one dealing with factors that all sociologists and historians must take into account, but it has assumed a special name, demography, organized its own scholarly associations, and assumed a considerable degree of autonomy. Formal demography is concerned with the size, composition, and geographical distribution of populations and with the processes of population change, principally fertility, mortality, and migration. Its data are largely of official origin and combine two broad types of material, one obtained by census enumerations of populations at a particular time, the other obtained by the continuous registration of certain events such as births, deaths, marriages, reportable diseases, and immigration and emigration.[55] The latter area of formal demography, concerned with the technical aspects of the col-

Znaniecki, *The Polish Peasant in Europe and America.* A useful recent comprehensive work is George E. Simpson and J. Milton Yinger, *Racial and Cultural Minorities* (New York: Harper & Brothers, 1953).

[52] See Gunnar Myrdal, Richard Sterner, and Arnold Rose, *An American Dilemma: The Negro Problem and Modern Democracy* (New York: Harper & Brothers, 1944), and Robin M. Williams, Jr., *The Reduction of Intergroup Tensions*, Social Science Research Council Bulletin 57 (New York, 1947).

[53] See Thorsten Sellin, *Culture Conflict and Crime*, Social Science Research Council Bulletin 41 (New York, 1938).

[54] Neither "criminology" nor "crime" appear in the indexes of the two recent general works cited in the present survey.

[55] The Committee was originally aided by Joseph J. Spengler, and later by Edward P. Hutchinson. For general discussion see U. S. National Resources Committee, *The Problems of a Changing Population* (Washington: Government Printing Office, 1938), and Frank Notestein and others, *The Future Population of Europe and the Soviet Union* (Geneva: League of Nations, 1944).

lection and analysis of registration data can be regarded as a sub-science in itself.[56]

Drawing its material largely from official sources, formal demography adopts many specialized terms and concepts directly from these sources, including such terms as family and household (as defined for census purposes), urban and rural, standard metropolitan area, still-birth, immigrant. Important supplementary information is also obtained from nonofficial research reports, but these for the most part employ accepted demographic terminology and definitions.

Demographers generally employ certain statistical terms and concepts, such as sex ratio (males per 100 females within a population), net migration, and birth and death rates "standardized" or adjusted for age composition of a population. From actuarial science come the term expectation of life and other terms related to the life table. The concept of replacement (that is, whether the fertility of a population is high enough to maintain its numbers) is important, and is most commonly measured by the net reproduction rate or index.[57]

Demographers are exploring increasingly beyond the descriptive and analytical aspects of formal demography and concerning themselves with the relations between population and other factors in human affairs, and especially with the explanation and implications of population phenomena. Thus, for example, demographic research over many years has accumulated considerable information about fertility differentials (intergroup differences in rate of reproduction); but only recently has attention turned to the questions of what social, economic, psychological or other influences produce these differentials, and what the implications or consequences of the differentials may be.

In the past demography has had close relations with certain natural and medical sciences such as statistics, biometry, epidemiology, and human geography. With wider interpretation of the scope of population studies, closer relations have been developed with the social

[56] See U. S. Bureau of the Census, *Handbook of Statistical Methods for Demographers: Selected Problems in the Analysis of Census Data,* preliminary edition by A. J. Jaffe (Washington, 1951); and Peter R. Cox, *Demography* (Cambridge: Cambridge University Press, 1950).

[57] The net reproduction rate of a population at a given period of time is derived from the age-specific fertility and mortality rates. The net reproduction rate can be described briefly as the estimated number of daughters that would be born to 100 newborn females subject throughout their lifetimes to the given fertility and mortality rates. If it is 100, then there is just replacement; if it is 110, for example, then there is an indicated 10 percent increase per generation.

sciences, particularly economics, sociology, and psychology; and the vocabulary and concepts of these fields have come into increasing use. One can also note an increase during the past decade or more in the number of historical studies of population.[58]

On the whole, however, except for occasional technical terms relating to specialized statistical techniques used in population study, demographic writings should be readily accessible to students from other fields, for demographers employ few terms or concepts not familiar in sociology or economics.

SOCIAL PSYCHOLOGY

In all explanations of human action, psychological considerations enter implicitly or explicitly at two points: first, in the diagnosis of the facts (abstraction of psychologically relevant features of the situation) and, second, in selection of explanatory principles. The inadequacies of scientific psychology make it inevitable that common sense assumptions, guided by wisdom and humanistic lore, must play a large part at both stages of interpretation. Explanation is more scientific, however, in the sense of successfully withstanding systematic doubt, to the extent that relevant concepts and principles of psychology are drawn upon when available, and common sense assumptions are subjected to explicit scrutiny.[59]

Common sense, in turn, continually acquires accretions from technical psychology and psychiatry, such as the concepts of inferiority complex, intelligence quotient, instinct, introversion, subconscious, repression, stimulus, and conditioned reflex. But these are likely to be fragments out of context, and their everyday use tends to sacrifice good English with no gain in precision. They may even be a pitfall in the way of satisfactory psychological interpretation.

Psychological concepts are valuable only within a theoretical context or frame of reference that includes explanatory principles. When appearances are to the contrary, analysis will usually show that implicit use is being made of unspecified principles. The historian who

[58] See, for example, Evarts B. Greene and Virginia D. Harrington, *American Population before the Federal Census of 1790* (New York: Columbia University Press, 1932); Stella H. Sutherland, *Population Distribution in Colonial America* (New York: Columbia University Press, 1936); and Josiah C. Russell, *British Medieval Population* (Albuquerque: University of New Mexico Press, 1948).

[59] Gardner Murphy and M. Brewster Smith each supplied a memorandum for the use of the Committee. These documents form the entire basis for this section, and no effort has been made to keep them separate.

wishes to refine and correct his common sense equipment by drawing on modern psychology must therefore not merely acquaint himself with a new and somewhat barbarous vocabulary; he must gain some sophistication in the frames of reference in which these terms are meaningful.[60]

The sharpest lines of cleavage in contemporary psychology divide areas of specialization and application rather than the schools of thought that played so prominent a role in the earlier history of the discipline.[61] Even though dogmatic loyalty to one or another competing comprehensive "system" is becoming a thing of the past and convergence is the order of the day, the alternative orientations from which psychologists seek to add to the common ground of empirically established knowledge are still best approached through their sources in the schools that dominated psychological theory in the 1920's: behaviorism, Gestalt, and psychoanalysis. Each in turn can be seen as one form taken by the reaction against the relatively sterile descriptive psychology of mental elements and compounds, which had its roots in British empiricist philosophy and which received a new experimental imprint from Wundt's laboratory in Leipzig.

Behaviorism in the era of its expounder, John B. Watson, was the outgrowth of an American "functionalist" revolt against the descriptive psychology of mental content. Impressed by the Darwinian emphasis on biological adaptation and utility, functionalists like the early John Dewey had shifted their focus from the content of experience to the processes of psychological functioning and their contribution to the economy of the organism. In 1919, in a widely read book, Watson ruled introspective accounts of consciousness out of court, to proclaim a harshly objective science that dealt solely with publicly observable behavior.[62] For the mental elements of sensation,

[60] For exemplary discussions see Solomon E. Asch, *Social Psychology* (New York: Prentice-Hall, 1952); Leon Festinger and Daniel Katz, eds., *Research Methods in the Behavioral Sciences* (New York: Dryden Press, 1953); Gardner Murphy, *Personality: A Biosocial Approach to Origins and Structure* (New York: Harper & Brothers, 1947); Theodore M. Newcomb, *Social Psychology* (New York: Dryden Press, 1950); and Guy E. Swanson, Theodore M. Newcomb, and Eugene L. Hartley, eds., *Readings in Social Psychology* (rev. ed.; New York: Henry Holt and Company, 1952).

[61] See Robert S. Woodworth, *Contemporary Schools of Psychology* (rev. ed.; New York: Ronald Press Company, 1948).

[62] John B. Watson, *Psychology from the Standpoint of a Behaviorist* (Philadelphia: J. B. Lippincott Company, 1919).

feeling, and imagery of the older school, the behaviorist substituted another set of elementary building blocks—first habits, and then, following the Russians Pavlov and Bekhterev, conditioned reflexes.

Historians may have had little occasion to find useful contact with the earlier behaviorism in its holy war against common sense views of conscious action. Newer, more sophisticated versions [63] leave room for mental processes, which now have the status not of directly observable primary facts but of inferences or "constructs" from observable data of behavior. It is, of course, as inferences or constructs that historians must reckon with mental phenomena if they are to do so at all. Nevertheless, the outgrowths of behaviorism are likely to concern historians only as exemplifying the psychologists' attempt at extreme rigor in research methodology and in systematic theory building. Since the behavioristic program moves from the simple to the complex only when the simple has been fully mastered, most behavioristic psychologists would probably agree that their contribution to the historian would be critical rather than constructive in the present stage of psychological knowledge.

Gestalt psychology, which originated in Germany and was transplanted to America largely in the post-Nazi emigration, revolted not against the mentalism of pre-Watsonian psychology but against its foundation in a doctrine of additive or compounded elements. In this respect it was equally in opposition to the elemental analysis of behavior by Watson and more modern behaviorists. The outstanding experimental contributions of the Gestalt movement have been to the psychology of perception and thought. Gestalt psychologists have characteristically stressed the intrinsic organization of mental processes, in which the part—like a note in a tune—takes its character and meaning from the whole composition.

Gestalt theory was the avenue through which the much broader philosophical movement of holism or organismic doctrine reached psychology. Outside the rather small and exclusive group of psychologists who identified themselves as Gestaltists, the influence of this holistic orientation as part of the intellectual current of the times is hard to distinguish from the impact of Gestalt psychology as such. The emphasis on organized systems of experience and behavior, on the complex determination of particular facts by the total structure in

[63] Clark L. Hull, *Principles of Behavior* (New York: D. Appleton-Century Co., 1943); Neal Miller and John Dollard, *Social Learning and Imitation* (New Haven: Yale University Press, 1941).

which they are embedded, as opposed to mechanical causal connections between intrinsically independent elements, is highly prevalent among students of personality and social psychology who claim no affiliation to strict Gestalt doctrine.

Kurt Lewin, a German psychologist with Gestalt affinities but not a member of the narrowly defined school, was particularly influential in giving impetus to this point of view in the areas of psychology bordering most closely on the other social sciences.[64] His approach is often identified as "field theory," from its emphasis on the determination of behavior by the person's entering a "psychological field"—the facts as psychologically relevant rather than as objectively discernible.

Such a "field" orientation, which contrasts most sharply with the objective frame of reference of modern behaviorists, starts its attempts to explain behavior with reconstruction of the actor's "private world." Convergent here are the psychoanalytic stress on the wishful or defensive shaping of perception and thought, the sociological tradition stemming from W. I. Thomas's discussion of the "definition of the situation," and the anthropological accounts of cultural selection from and phrasing of objective reality. The historian perhaps has little to learn here from what he may regard as the rediscovery of the obvious. But by using scientific concepts he will find communication easier with psychologists who share this orientation.

Freud originated psychoanalysis in a medical context, and in its formative period it was isolated from academic psychology. In spite of a certain reaction against its bizarre terminology, ornate constructions, sexual focus, and general lack of scientific confirmation, psychologists have increasingly come to attribute the greatest importance to Freud's discoveries. For one thing, they filled what was a conspicuous vacuum in psychology—the theory of motivation. Prior to the influence of psychoanalysis, psychology had nothing satisfactory to offer to those who expected it to provide an account of the why's of human behavior. From his studies of psychopathology, dreams, and human error Freud gained insights concerning the vicissitudes of motives, whatever their source, under the impact of society, and so put a corrective emphasis on the nonrational components of human behavior.[65]

[64] See Kurt Lewin, *A Dynamic Theory of Personality* (trans. Donald K. Adams and Karl E. Zener; New York: McGraw-Hill Book Company, 1935); and *Resolving Social Conflicts* (D. O. Cartwright, ed.; New York: Harper & Brothers, 1948).
[65] See Clara Thompson, *Psychoanalysis: Evolution and Development* (New York:

Among the important insights for which psychology is indebted to Freud, the following may serve as illustrations: the considerable extent to which persons act in terms of coherent purposes that lie outside the range of awareness, in what is called the unconscious or, expressed in another way, the extent to which apparently bizarre, nonrational behavior—dreams, symptoms, mistakes, and slips of the tongue—is meaningful in the sense of being directed toward a goal of which the actor is not consciously aware. In this connection Freud and his followers have identified various novel forms that mental processes may take when proceeding unconsciously and excluded from critical scrutiny. These include: *ambivalence,* which refers to opposite feelings coexisting toward the same object; *displacement,* a process in which the emotions appropriate to but not permitted toward one object are evoked by another; *condensation,* a process in which a thought, expression, or act carries a multiplicity of meanings through the several contexts with which it is associatively linked; and finally, *projection,* a process in which one's own repressed qualities or motives are attributed to others.

To describe the defensive or adjustive processes by which the individual fends off anxiety from inner or outer sources, Freudian psychologists have developed certain concepts of which historians should be aware, if only to avoid misusing them. These include *projection,* as just described; *repression,* or exclusion from conscious awareness; *reaction formation,* essentially "leaning over backward," the development of a pattern of behavior suitable to the situation as it is consciously interpreted, but opposed to an impulse at the unconscious level; *isolation,* or the separation of thoughts from their emotional accompaniments or their anxiety-producing contexts; and *rationalization,* or the invention of plausible and acceptable reasons for unconsciously motivated behavior. Freudians stress the importance of family relationships in infancy and early childhood in establishing the basis of adult "character structure," and in particular the process of *identification* with parental figures as the source of conscience (the superego) and, ultimately, of cultural continuity in social control.

Developments in psychoanalysis since Freud have retained this core of "psychodynamics," but so-called neo-Freudians like Karen Horney

Hermitage House, 1950); and Ernest Jones, *The Life and Work of Sigmund Freud* (New York: Basic Books, 1953). An illustrative work by Freud is *Civilization and Its Discontents* (trans. Joan Riviere; New York: Jonathan Cape & Harrison Smith, 1930). See also *The Basic Writings of Sigmund Freud* (New York: Modern Library, 1938).

and Erich Fromm have rejected the biological assumptions of libido theory (the dominant importance of the sexual drive and its assumed transformations) and have attempted to assimilate into psychoanalysis the theories of sociology and cultural anthropology regarding the cultural and social determination of many factors that Freud believed to be biologically foreordained.[66] Even within the group of orthodox psychoanalysts, recent developments in what they term "ego psychology" have shifted the emphasis from the realm of irrational urge and wish (the id) to that of the constructive operations of personality in mediating between wish and outer reality (the ego).

The study of personality, which has an obvious interest for historians, has been markedly influenced by both psychoanalytic and holistic currents of thought; the two converge in a concern with personality structure and have replaced the earlier attempt to account for it in terms of separate elements.

Social psychology has a past in both psychology and sociology; the two lines of development are increasingly merging in research and writing. Psychologists, however, have usually regarded the two as separate but related special fields. Although it has a fairly long speculative history, social psychology became the active field of empirical research that it is today only in the years immediately preceding World War II.

"Theory in social psychology was long torn between stress on the isolated individual, who somehow had to be related to others to form a society, and on a reified society or group, the basis of which in individual psychological processes then became most mysterious." [67] Compelled by its self-imposed charter to deal with the bridge between individual and group concepts, social psychological theory underwent a series of gyrations reflecting the tensions generated by undertaking an impossible task. A hopeful recent development, therefore, is the emergence from diverse quarters of incipient consensus on a model, itself by no means new, that rejects this troublesome dichotomy of isolated individual versus disembodied group.

In its minimal features this model or frame of reference starts not from individuals or sociocultural entities but from the interactions of

[66] See Erich Fromm, *Escape from Freedom* (New York: Farrar & Rinehart, 1941); and Clara Thompson, *op. cit.*

[67] M. Brewster Smith, "Anthropology and Psychology," in John Gillin, ed., *For a Science of Social Man* (New York: Macmillan Company, 1954), p. 64. This and the following three paragraphs are adapted from *ibid.*, pp. 64–65, by permission.

persons; hence it is sometimes called "interactionism." In any functioning social group, according to this view, the so-called isolated individual is a misleading fiction. Persons achieve communication and
avoid randomness in their relationships because each already embodies
in his personality much of the sociocultural system in microcosm. That
is, the symbol systems, beliefs, and expectations of each other's actions
shared by members of a social group, and the modified or emergent
motives, aspirations, and standards of evaluation learned in group
experience, so transform man as a biological entity that he exists
always in implicit relation to others. The notion of men as social
atoms which are somehow to be brought into significant relation to
one another is simply a myth, except when applied to collections of
infants.

With the demise of the isolated individual, the case for social
realism—the "group mind," or culture as "superorganic"—loses its
pertinence. More, to be sure, than the sum of its individual members
taken separately, a group is essentially a set of interacting persons and
their relationships without the necessity for any *tertium quid*.

Developmentally the model suggests that, in and through the process
of social interaction, the actor *learns* to become the sort of person who
is capable of the orderly social relationships in which he later par-
ticipates. The conditions and consequences of the socialization process,
as "learning" in this context is termed, become therefore a central
problem for research. Through socialization, culture, which at the
outset of the life cycle is exterior to the person and constraining upon
him, becomes internalized—inextricably incorporated in his very
make-up. Yet while the person takes on the culture in which he is
raised, he assimilates it in his own idiosyncratic version. And since
culture exists only in the shared practices and understandings among
the members of a social group, he contributes to cultural innovation
and change at the same time that he sustains cultural continuity.[68] To
contemporary social psychologists the controversy between the "great
man" and the economic or cultural interpretations of history rests upon
a false dichotomy.

The significance of this new theoretical orientation can be seen in
a field with major historical relevance—the psychology of leadership.
Psychologists formerly sought to find in leaders a specific set of qualities, perhaps distinguishable as a personality type. Today it is generally
agreed that leadership is a relation to which the leader, the follower,

[68] See Barnett, *Innovation*.

and the requirements of the situation, including the traditions of the group, all contribute. The leader has a social role, defined by the behavior expected of him by the members of his group, and this role interlocks with reciprocal roles of other group members.[69] His personal qualities and actual behavior enable him to satisfy the requirements of this role more or less successfully.

Since the 1930's psychologists and psychoanalysts have joined cultural anthropologists in a focal interest in culture and personality—although these terms are infelicitous in suggesting external relations between two independent entities, rather than a belated attempt to bring together two abstractions from social behavior that can be isolated only artificially. Case studies of personality development in a number of nonliterate "primitive" societies, selected to exemplify a wide range of social practice, suggest complex relationships between the traditional cultural beliefs and practices in which individuals are reared and the features of personality most frequently found among members of a society. Various scholars have employed essentially synonymous terms, such as basic personality structure, modal personality, social character, and national character, for the underlying features of personality organization common to or most frequent among the members of a social group.[70] It has been suggested that personality structure provides a mediating link between apparently unrelated features of culture that nonetheless hang together, as when a people like the Hopi among whom overt expression of hostility is culturally disapproved also manifest a highly developed set of beliefs in malevolent sorcery, which according to psychoanalytic assumptions provides an outlet for the displaced discharge of aggressive impulses.

Knowledge of the interrelations of culture and personality is closer to the level of clinical insight than of systematic validation, although considerable research is concerned with these problems. The historian may be especially interested in the work on national character carried out under wartime and defense restrictions that enforce reliance on indirect, often documentary, evidence. Although standards of rigor have not been very high in this field, provocative suggestions may be found for research on earlier historical periods.[71]

69 Cf. pp. 49–51, *supra.*

70 See Erich Fromm, *op. cit.;* and Abram Kardiner and others, *The Psychological Frontiers of Society* (New York: Columbia University Press, 1945).

71 See Margaret Mead, *Soviet Attitudes toward Authority* (New York: McGraw-Hill Book Company, 1952); Margaret Mead and Rhoda Métraux, eds., *The Study of Culture at a Distance* (Chicago: University of Chicago Press, 1953).

In recent years the study of personality has drawn on the use of so-called projective techniques. While the validity of particular techniques remains to be established, clinical psychologists think they can infer much about how a person organizes his "private world" and about his motives from what he makes of such ambiguous or "unstructured" tasks as to see pictures in inkblots (Rorschach Test), or to make up dramatic stories about pictures (Thematic Apperception Test). The same kind of interpretative strategy has been employed with literary productions and other personal documents accessible to the historian and biographer.[72]

If adult personality types seen in the culture are to be understood, psychological growth processes should also be studied in terms of early family influences and methods of childhood training, because it is in the earliest and most formative years that the social environment reacts strongly upon the developing personality, including the unconscious dynamics to which psychoanalysis refers.

As already noted, the individual member of a group is profoundly guided in his perception, recall, and thought by both the social-cultural factors and personal factors of the sort that led an older generation to speak of "wishful thinking" and that are now called autistic. Experimental studies of autistic response have been very prominent since the early 1930's. H. A. Murray's studies in the Harvard Psychological Clinic initiated a wave of investigation showing the personal dynamics of perception; showing, indeed, that nobody can write a document either about himself or about anybody else without its being profoundly colored and biased by the unconscious as well as conscious aspects of what he himself is; nor can safety be found in numbers, because men trained within a given culture or within a given school cannot, by any possible mechanism, serve as adequate balances to one another.[73]

In most societies or groups, status differentials give rise to strivings for status and to characteristic techniques for preserving status. Because an individual belongs to many groups, such as family, occupational, or national, he often has many roles to play, some of which

---

[72] See Gordon Allport, *The Use of Personal Documents in Psychological Science,* and Louis Gottschalk, Clyde Kluckhohn, and Robert Angell, *The Use of Personal Documents in History, Anthropology, and Sociology,* Social Science Research Council Bulletins 49 and 53 (New York, 1942, 1945).

[73] See Clyde Kluckhohn, Henry A. Murray, and David M. Schneider, eds., *Personality in Nature, Society, and Culture* (2nd ed.; New York: Alfred A. Knopf, 1953).

are more satisfying than others. In the frequently occurring, ambiguous situations where the reference group [74] is not clearly specified and the role involvement consequently is not defined, autistic elements operate to make the individual see the situation in a way favorable to his own strivings.

Deviations from the social norm of role behavior have been studied and classified in a manner that if valid has many implications for the study of social change.[75] It is suggested that there are two negative deviations: rejection of the socially expected role; and outward acceptance of the role but inability to function successfully in it. The delinquent who rejects the culturally acceptable roles would illustrate the first; the man who tries to support the position of a political party against his own beliefs, the second. A third type of deviation is qualitatively entirely different and may be considered a positive deviation. It takes the form of carrying out the spirit or purpose of the role without regard to the customary pattern of behavior expected in one performing the particular functions, as in the case of a bold political reformer. It is in this type of deviation from role that constructive leadership emerges, and change and novelty are introduced.

Certain biographical techniques in which some knowledge of clinical psychological methods is represented are well worth the historian's attention. Faced with the task of constructing an interpretive biography, the investigator trained in psychological methods would formulate hypotheses as he started work on the early life of his subject—hypotheses as to what sort of person the man would prove to be when he later became involved in different types of situations. A systematic testing of these hypotheses against the evidence provided at different stages in the life history would not only provide clues to the understanding of motives but would also focus the biography sharply on the processes of personality development. Also important in biography are description and analysis of the behavior of the individual in terms of the social roles played by him, the structure of the various organized systems of interaction in which he found himself, and the patterns of sanctions to which he was exposed in playing those roles. Close attention to possible conflicts between different roles or different patterns of sanctions may frequently suggest explanations for otherwise inexplicable kinds of behavior. Above all, the personality

---

[74] See p. 51, *supra.*
[75] See Adam Curle and E. L. Trist, "Transitional Communities and Social Reconnection," *Human Relations,* 1:42–68, 240–288 (1947).

of the actor should be regarded as part of the problem to be investigated, not as something "given." The analysis of motivation, in particular, presents great methodological difficulties which demand the most rigorous use of evidence and hypotheses. Explanations of the behavior of an individual in terms of certain personal qualities imputed to him without independent evidence as to how he acquired or developed such qualities do not constitute sound practice, if only for the reason that they cannot be proved or disproved.

POLITICAL SCIENCE

Since political events are still the usual backbone of historical synthesis, historians are inclined to think that they are already conversant with the field of government or political science. True in general of earlier generations, the assumption is no longer valid. Within the last twenty years political scientists have been absorbing interests and techniques from anthropology, sociology, and social psychology, and undertaking new types of research. Unlike those three social sciences, however, political science is concerned only with a selected group of social processes, which it treats with particular reference to the formation of policy and the making of decisions carrying coercive sanctions. Within this scope, political science has developed by means of three principal methods: normative theory, institutional analysis, and process analysis.[76]

Viewed in terms of general concepts, the interests of political scientists relate in one way or another to *power*. This concept serves principally as a rough means of defining the area of concern and identifying the political element in human relations. As a substantive concept power may be regarded as approximately equivalent to authority, formal or informal. As a relational concept, power amounts virtually to the process of government.

Attention is focused on another aspect of the phenomena of politics through use of the concept of decision making. But in actions ranging from the formation of constitutions to the punishment of violators of traffic ordinances, the decisions are influenced by power

[76] Material for this section has been supplied by David Easton, Oliver Garceau, V. O. Key, and E. E. Schattschneider. As in other sections, use has been made of their manuscripts without specific acknowledgment. For a good introduction to the problems of research in political science, see Avery Leiserson, "Problems of Methodology in Political Science," *Political Science Quarterly*, 68:558–584 (December 1953).

relationships. Governmental decisions are supported by sanctions that depend ultimately on the monopoly of force claimed by the state. This is perhaps the critical factor in the formal demarcation of the area of behavior that is of concern to political scientists. These observations point to limitations on power (processes of government) as an organizing concept, for power relations exist independent of the apparatus of the state. Although no consensus prevails on the question, many political scientists are disposed to take into account relationships not immediately involving the machinery of the state to describe the structure of power in a particular society; the necessity for so catholic a concern depends, of course, on the nature of the particular political system under examination.[77]

But in one way or another, directly or indirectly, political research has to deal with the determinants of *public policy*.[78] It has to show how and why the activities, institutions, and structure of a society give rise to one kind of policy rather than another. Each field of research in political science seeks to discover the important determinants in the formulation and execution of public policy. For example, in the study of national and comparative government, political scientists seek to understand the ways in which certain institutional activities, such as those of legislatures or executives, influence the kind of policies adopted. In the study of public administration they are concerned primarily with the social determinants governing the execution of formal policies.

Rigorously defined, the concept of public policy refers to every deliberate allocation of values by a society. Whenever a government acts to distribute certain desirable or undesirable things (values) in a society in a given way or states that they are to be so allocated, we have the existence of a policy for that society. The formal aspect of the policy is the statement of intent. Normally this takes the form of a law, executive order, directive, or administrative rule. But a policy,

[77] See Pendleton Herring, *The Politics of Democracy* (New York: W. W. Norton & Company, 1940); David Easton, *The Political System: An Inquiry into the State of Political Science* (New York: Alfred A. Knopf, 1953); and United Nations Educational, Scientific and Cultural Organization, *Contemporary Political Science*, UNESCO Publication No. 426 (Paris, 1950).

[78] See Charles E. Merriam, *Systematic Politics* (Chicago: University of Chicago Press, 1945); Ernest S. Griffith, ed., *Research in Political Science* (Chapel Hill: University of North Carolina Press, 1948); Harold D. Lasswell and Abraham Kaplan, *Power and Society: A Framework for Political Inquiry* (New Haven: Yale University Press, 1950).

as is well known, consists of more than intention; it has an effective aspect as well. The actual way in which the formal policy is put into effect is also part of the policy, even though the effective policy may modify, subvert, or even destroy the formal enunciation of intention. Public policy, accordingly, is a concept that refers simultaneously to the formal and effective or actual allocation of values for a society.

The political scientist strives to identify the competing values that seek validation in organized government, traces their historical origins and mutations, and relates them to social groupings in historical context.[79] Hence, political theory may often be differentiated only with difficulty from political philosophy. The latter tries to establish moral criteria for determining what the goals or policies of a society should be in order to satisfy the precepts of the given philosophy. As in sociology a coordinated system of political beliefs is called an ideology, for example, democratic ideology, communist ideology. The term myth is often employed in a kindred manner to denote the faith or system of values and beliefs that permeates a society. This use of the term myth usually involves the assumption that the structure of power or the system of authority derives vitality from general acceptance of the values and ends embodied in the dominant ideology of the society.

If the normative work of political science has been closely associated with the method of philosophy, much of the institutional work has been in the tradition of the law. In studies of constitutional and administrative law, political science works toward a systematic statement of formal, legally binding decisions, involving both their substance and the requirements for their validity.

On a comparative basis, political science examines the major political institutions in the subcultures of the Western nation states.[80] Institutions are compared tentatively to determine consequences in terms of normative values and of the quality and adequacy of policy decisions produced. Little comparative analysis has been attempted beyond the literate and industrial states of the West. The multiplicity of variables introduced into the analysis, even within the relatively homogeneous Western states, and the paucity of cases available mili-

[79] See Carl J. Friedrich, *Constitutional Government and Democracy* (rev. ed.; Boston: Ginn and Company, 1950); Alexander D. Lindsay, *The Modern Democratic State* (New York: Oxford University Press, 1947); and Charles H. McIlwain, *The Growth of Political Thought in the West* (New York: Macmillan Company, 1932).

[80] See Herman Finer, *Theory and Practice of Modern Government* (rev. ed.; New York: Henry Holt and Company, 1949).

tate against the development of a rigorous causal theory dealing with major political institutions.

In the comparison of institutions, attempts are made to isolate and analyze the operating results of particular institutional forms, although the identification of the critical variables remains imprecise. One type of institutional study has as its focus the processes of institutional behavior, such as legislative process or judicial process. Process analysis may be extended to long-term phenomena (for example, to the process of centralization or that of executive aggrandizement) or it may center on particular institutions or on the comparative analysis of institutions in similar or different cultures.[81]

In other social sciences the concept of process refers to change over time or the activities within a structure, but political scientists normally use the concept to identify every kind of activity, structured or otherwise, that plays a part in shaping public policy. Political process is equivalent to the idea of the interaction of all political variables viewed as a complex totality.

A dichotomy of some utility in the description of political analysis is that between studies of the formal institutions of government and the informal processes of attaining and retaining authority. A similar distinction is that between legal and extralegal or constitutional and extraconstitutional aspects of the process of government.[82] These processes, by virtue of being informal, occur in great variety. Some areas of analysis relate to political conditioning factors, such as the nature and structure of the economy, the social class structure, religious beliefs, doctrines of political faith, or culture. In other areas attention is centered on the actors or interest groups influencing or participating in the struggle for control of government.[83]

At present, studies of political process and institutions are largely culture-bound and deal only with segments of patterns of social interaction. They show promise, however, of achieving a greater degree of generalization, sufficient to permit the development and testing of hypotheses applicable to a political system in its totality. Studies of

[81] David B. Truman, *The Governmental Process: Political Interests and Public Opinion* (New York: Alfred A. Knopf, 1951).

[82] See Stephen K. Bailey, *Congress Makes a Law* (New York: Columbia University Press, 1950); and E. E. Schattschneider, *Politics, Pressures and the Tariff* (New York: Prentice-Hall, 1935).

[83] See V. O. Key, *Southern Politics in State and Nation* (New York: Alfred A. Knopf, 1949); and E. E. Schattschneider, *Party Government* (New York: Rinehart & Company, 1942).

process have emphasized group analysis and the force of social sanctions; intergroup bargaining, communication, and voting behavior have also received considerable attention.

Administration, regarded as the process of executing policy, has become a special field of political science with its own body of terminology, which serves to describe administrative structure and aids in the rapid formation of new administrative agencies. The concept of hierarchy, with staff and line used to denote sub-units of hierarchy with particular functions and relations, is still of basic importance. In recent years, however, the rather static structural analysis of administration has been supplemented through recognition of the role of informal groups and informal relationships in the behavior of persons hierarchically situated.[84] One approach to the analysis of administration focuses on the administrative process and includes attention to the internal division of labor, the relations between and within agencies, the procedures for obtaining information on which to base decisions, and practices in the review of decisions to prevent abuse of power and to assure conformity with law.

Another specialized interest of political science is international relations. Here political theory, institutional analysis, and administration are generally fused with history. Diplomatic history and international relations are separated, if at all, merely by the span of time under consideration. But the historian in this field may profit from studying the political scientist's systematic patterns of analysis.[85]

ECONOMICS

Economics deals essentially with the patterns of behavior involved in the allocation of scarce resources among alternative uses. Its central problem is that of *value:* this is conventionally broken up into theories of production, distribution, employment, prices and exchange. In addition economists have developed special fields of study such as business fluctuations, entrepreneurship, and economic growth.[86] Eco-

[84] Herbert A. Simon, *Administrative Behavior* (New York: Macmillan Company, 1947); and William Anderson and John M. Gaus, *Research in Public Administration* (Chicago: Public Administration Service, 1945).

[85] See Werner Levi, *Fundamentals of World Organization* (Minneapolis: University of Minnesota Press, 1950); and Hans J. Morgenthau, *Politics Among Nations* (New York: Alfred A. Knopf, 1948).

[86] A. G. Hart served as the Committee's consultant in economics. For general guidance see *A Survey of Contemporary Economics*, Vol. I–II, *op. cit.* Since the

nomic hypotheses and models rest on assumptions regarding social action, and they are developed by simplifying assumptions regarding certain variables selected from the general complex of human behavior. For example, the rate of growth of an economy, no matter how measured, is the product of a multitude of factors, but for inclusion in a model it may be treated as a single constant or variable. Since the ways in which the economic functions are carried on are inter-related parts of the society's total structure, the economist faces the major dilemma of all social theory, that of devising models simple enough to manipulate, but still approximately representative of complex reality.

To a much greater degree than the other social sciences, economics in the nineteenth century developed a coherent body of theory. This "classical theory" assumed man's economic activity to be more uniformly motivated and hence more predictable than all or most other aspects of his behavior. In economic affairs man was presumed to act rationally in the sense of trying to maximize satisfaction and minimize effort. From this supposition plus the concept that the economy tended to maintain an equilibrium it was possible to deduce theorems regarding economic behavior.[87]

The questioning of the assumption of hedonistic economic man by other social sciences in the twentieth century led to the formal abandonment of this basic assumption, but it was implicitly retained in much theorizing. T. W. Hutchison says of this situation: "[It is not] the case that the foundations of economic science have been found necessarily to be precarious, but rather that it is not at all clear . . . what they are."[88] This, however, does not prevent additional theory building since "Purely theoretical analysis consists in the manipulation of concepts in accordance with the rules laid down in their definitions. The assigning of definitions, therefore, obviously plays a key role in the construction of pure theory. . . . The *applicability* of the assumptions . . . may be criticised; but this is purely a question of fact,

---

concepts in economics are highly refined and technical, a beginner may wish to consult a general survey, such as Paul A. Samuelson, *Foundations of Economic Analysis* (Cambridge: Harvard University Press, 1947).

[87] The best summary of this view is in Alfred Marshall, *Principles of Economics* (London: Macmillan and Co., 1890, and many later editions). See also Charles Gide and Charles Rist, *A History of Economic Doctrines from the Time of the Physiocrats to the Present Day* (London: G. G. Harrop & Co., 1948).

[88] T. W. Hutchison, *The Significance and Basic Postulates of Economic Theory* (London: Macmillan and Co., 1938), p. 4.

having nothing to do with the *form* of a proposition of pure theory, which *must* necessarily be 'tautological,' 'circular,' and 'assume what it proves'—for what it proves must be contained in the assumptions, and cannot be obtained from any other source." [89]

If one assumes, for example, that a perfect market is one in which there are so many buyers and sellers each dealing in such small quantities that the action of no one buyer or seller affects the price more than infinitesimally, then a host of corollaries can be drawn regarding the behavior of such a market. Other initial assumptions may be made, leading to different corollaries. But the premises do not state that such a market has ever existed in reality.

To illustrate the processes of deductive theorizing we may cite Paul A. Samuelson's statement that all useful theorems in economics can be derived from two hypotheses: First, the equilibrium position of prices, quantities, etc. represents a *maximum* position for some magnitude such as utility or profits; if this is true, then the characteristics of the economic system can be developed from the secondary conditions for a maximum. Second, an equilibrium position represents a *stable* situation in the sense that slight deviations tend to be self-corrective.[90]

One notes the introduction of mathematical (symbolic) logic in deriving the secondary conditions for a maximum. Reliance on mathematical reasoning has made possible both more elaborate structures of pure theory, and the introduction of movement as a factor. Dynamic economics, for example, is based on the projection, largely by mathematical means, of present assumptions into the future. The term econometrics is used in general to indicate the application of mathematical and statistical techniques to economic problems.

Pure theory as such is obviously of limited use to the historian. As Sir John Clapham wrote many years ago: "The central problems of economic theory, although they may be stated in terms of a particular historical phase, are in essence independent of history." [91] Ordinarily the data used by historians are not expressible in theoretical equations, and even when this is possible historians are usually unwilling to eliminate the force of other factors not included in the

[89] *Ibid.*, pp. 30, 36.
[90] Samuelson, *op. cit.*, p. 5.
[91] Quoted in Frederic C. Lane and Jelle C. Riemersma, eds., *Enterprise and Secular Change: Readings in Economic History* (Homewood, Ill.: Richard D. Irwin, 1953), p. 419.

theorem. Pure theory has important values, however. It defines logically the interests of economists and the boundaries of their field, it stimulates the imagination and leads to new investigations, and it reminds the historian of the inadequacy of mere description.

Recognizing the difficulties inherent in using deductive propositions for empirical research, some American economists of the late nineteenth century discarded British classicism in favor of a version of the empirically based German "historical" school. The American approach came to be called "institutional" or, by some recent writers, "holistic" economics.[92] From the 1920's on, the National Bureau of Economic Research and its leading spirit, Wesley C. Mitchell, undertook studies of national income and the business cycle from the institutional point of view.[93] Institutional economists favor setting up a minimum of tentative hypotheses in advance of the research, and elaborating them only as the evidence suggests. As the historian well knows, such a process generally produces few adequately tested hypotheses, and coherent theory grows slowly.

Whereas the institutionalists rejected classical theory, except for its terminology, other economists have sought to modify classical theory in order to make it fit the conditions of large-scale industrialism. This has given rise to a number of deductions regarding the causal role of price movements, a rethinking of the mechanics of the market, such as the theory of monopolistic competition, and new assumptions regarding conditions of economic equilibrium.[94] A modification of classicism that has had strong repercussions on public policy was brought about by John Maynard Keynes. He attacked the assumption that full employment was the normal or equilibrium position of the economy. He suggested new factors determining the level of national

[92] See John R. Commons, *Institutional Economics* (New York: Macmillan Company, 1934); John M. Clark, *Preface to Social Economics* (New York: Farrar & Rinehart, 1936); Wesley C. Mitchell, ed., *What Veblen Taught* (New York: Viking Press, 1936).

[93] Wesley C. Mitchell, *The National Bureau's First Quarter-Century*, National Bureau of Economic Research, Twenty-Fifth Annual Report (New York, 1945).

[94] Irving Fisher, *The Purchasing Power of Money* (New York: Macmillan Company, 1922); Alvin H. Hansen, *Fiscal Policy and Business Cycles* (New York: W. W. Norton & Company, 1941); Edward H. Chamberlin, *The Theory of Monopolistic Competition* (6th ed.; Cambridge: Harvard University Press, 1948); Arthur R. Burns, *The Decline of Competition* (New York: McGraw-Hill Book Company, 1936); and George J. Stigler, *The Theory of Price* (rev. ed.; New York: Macmillan Company, 1952).

income, and drew attention to the importance of government fiscal policy as the regulator of employment and investment.[95]

All schools of economics, however, share certain general orientations. They believe in the desirability of quantification and examination of the behavior of aggregates; for this the chief technique is the construction of statistics measuring some phenomenon at regular intervals, called a time series. The direction of movement in such a series over long periods is known as a secular trend. All schools, too, agree fairly well on the boundaries of economic analysis. This agreement comes partly from the common acceptance of most of the concepts and terms of nineteenth century classical theory, particularly as stated by Alfred Marshall at the end of the century. The historian should be familiar with this widely accepted language of economics.

Natural resources, often simplified as "land," labor, technology, and capital, are spoken of as the factors of production. A process in which the cost per unit produced falls as the volume of production increases is called one of decreasing or diminishing cost. Most industrial processes are of this type over a considerable range of output. Decreasing cost aids the firm that produces a larger volume than its competitors and is consequently a powerful factor in economic change.

Agricultural production is often referred to as primary, industrial as secondary, and services as tertiary. Since the level of secondary and tertiary production depends mainly on the number of workers who can be spared from producing food, an increase in these later stages is sometimes taken as an index of economic progress.

The economist plots varying relations between economic factors in graphic curves—cost curves, demand curves, supply curves, and many others. A "curve" results from plotting the functions of two variables (such as $x^2 - y^2 = 10$), and it has become common in recent years to speak of a graphic line representing some measure of production as a production function, a graphic representation of consumption as a consumption function, and so on.

It is assumed that an entrepreneur (one who makes the decisions necessary for conducting a business unit) combines the factors of production in such a way as to maximize profit over some period of

[95] The primary statement of Keynes' ideas is in *The General Theory of Employment, Interest and Money* (New York: Harcourt, Brace and Company, 1936), but historians will find it easier to learn the general principles of "Keynesianism" from Dudley Dillard, *The Economics of John Maynard Keynes* (New York: Prentice-Hall, 1948).

time. The "classic" hypothesis governing the combination is that units of each factor will be added until the contribution to total revenue of the last unit added just covers its cost. The last unit added is said to be the marginal unit, and its cost the marginal cost. Similarly one may derive such concepts as marginal revenue or marginal productivity. The rules for profit maximization that can be developed by the use of these concepts are precise abstract deductions that cannot take account of such factors as uncertainty, personal aims, social pressures, or faulty communication.

Common sense or experience indicates that as any factor of production is increased relative to the other factors, a point must finally be reached where there are diminishing returns in output relative to the added input. During periods of unusual demand, such as a war or an inflationary boom, goods may be produced for a while under such conditions of diminishing returns. A firm, which is assumed to be trying to maximize its profits, however, will try to produce at the level of minimum average cost, a level below the point where diminishing returns become evident. When elements of monopoly are strong, the firm may maximize its profits at an output smaller than the one that would lead to minimum average cost.

The specialization of workers in limited productive operations is known as "division of labor" and is assumed to increase productive efficiency. The use of machinery, growth in size of markets, and increase in scale of operations tend to promote division of labor. Such economic deductions are, of course, not concerned with the possibility that narrow specialization may work against social efficiency or welfare.

Capital is conceived as anything having exchange market value that can be employed in the production of other things having exchange value. One convenient way of distinguishing various forms of capital is in terms of liquidity, or in other words the ease with which they can be converted into freely disposable resources. In these terms, money is the most liquid form of capital, stocks of raw materials are less liquid, and actual productive equipment, such as a blast furnace or a hydraulic press, less liquid still. Capital is used in almost all productive processes and is not restricted to the form of social organization called "capitalism." Even a fisherman in a primitive society needs a line or a net, and these are capital or, stated so as to distinguish them from money, they are capital goods. Since capital goods are those used for further production, they are sometimes called production goods. Goods that may be used over and over again such as table silver are called durable goods, and those like clothes that can be used at least a number of times are semi-durable goods. But not all durable goods are capital. A business automobile is capital, but a pleasure car is properly classified as a consumer durable, that is, it is not "employed in the production of other things having exchange value."

The location of a productive unit is determined in theory by the search for the situation that will give minimum average costs per unit of output. Particularly important are costs of transport of raw materials and finished products, but factors such as labor and land costs are also relevant. Recent empirical research has indicated many other relevant factors such as residence of the entrepreneur, local financial interests, local buying habits, and the availability of special labor or managerial skills. Hypotheses regarding the probable relation of these factors that will determine where a business will be located or when it will be moved to a new site are called location theory. Since such hypotheses seek to explain important types of social movement, they are of interest to the historian.[96]

Distribution is used technically to refer to the division of the income of an enterprise between the various factors of production, and popularly to refer to the processes by which goods and services reach the consumer. The latter meaning will be avoided in this discussion.

The net share of the returns allotted to the owner or owners of the capital ventured in an enterprise is profit, but accountants and economists have many theories regarding the proper basis for such allotment, and as a result the concept of profit lacks a single precise definition.

Savings are the part of corporate or private income that is not spent for taxes or consumption. They may initially take the form of hoarded currency, bank deposits, insurance and annuity premiums, or the purchase of securities. The relations between saving and investment in capital goods are regarded differently by various schools. The classic view is that all saving that reaches the financial markets results in investment in real goods or services. Some scholars, such as the followers of Keynes, hold that investment in actual capital goods may

96 See Carl J. Friedrich, *Alfred Weber's Theory of the Location of Industries* (Chicago: University of Chicago Press, 1929); and Edgar M. Hoover, *The Location of Economic Activity* (New York: McGraw-Hill Book Company, 1948).

or may not occur depending upon the use made of the savings by intermediary agencies. The argument hinges on the length of time that savings can be held back from labor-employing investment by purely financial manipulations and involves complicated problems that cannot be discussed here.[97]

Increments of income taken from consumers without their volition are called forced savings. A bankrupt firm has "forced" its creditors to contribute. Similarly the sharp rise in prices characteristic of periods of inflation produces forced savings on the part of persons with fixed incomes and others whose income grows less rapidly than the rate of price increase. These persons are forced to restrict their consumption, thus freeing scarce resources, which would ordinarily be used to supply normal consumer demand, for use elsewhere. These situations also involve complexities that cannot be explored here, but the historian should note that much of the capital accumulation of societies has always come from forced rather than voluntary savings.[98]

The study of exchange is subdivided into several specialties. The distribution of goods to consumers, assumed in classic theory to be governed by economic "laws," is now called marketing, and involves psychological and sociological research in such matters as communication and consumer preferences. As already noted, the market in the theory of pure competition is a meeting place for the buyers and sellers of uniform goods, in which the number of both buyers and sellers is so large that no one sale or purchase has a noticeable effect on price. Such relations would require no empirical study of marketing. But in practice markets are imperfect. Large buyers or sellers influence price by more or less concerted action, or what appears to be one market may on closer analysis be revealed to be a number of separate but overlapping markets. For example, there is not just one market for automobiles, but an overlapping series on the basis of the price ranges possible for consumers of varying wealth. To take an extreme case, a purchaser may be willing and able to pay between $300 and $800 for a used car without severe sacrifices in other parts of his budget, but it would probably be impossible for him to enter the market for a $4,000 car. Theoretical assumptions about the effects

[97] See Morris A. Copeland, *A Study of Moneyflows in the United States* (New York: National Bureau of Economic Research, 1952).

[98] Earl J. Hamilton, "Prices as a Factor in Business Growth," *Journal of Economic History*, 12:325–349 (Fall 1952).

of market imperfections are grouped under the heading of monopolistic competition, and offer an excellent example of the value of
pure theory in suggesting probable relations in the real world.

The aim of the producer in seeking to establish conditions of
monopolistic competition is assumed to be to secure a higher or
more certain profit than would be secured with free competition. One
logical way of doing this is to make his products appear to differ
from those of his competitors, and so to establish a special market
for his wares. In theory this is called product differentiation, and in
the real world it is seen in the advertising of superior qualities,
attractive packaging, or special features not common to the products
of competitors. The soapmakers, for example, try all these devices and
thereby create a group of consumers who prefer to buy a certain
brand even though its price may be as high as or higher than the price
of a competing brand. Conversely, the existence of product differentiation is taken as an indication that elements of monopolistic competition
exist in that particular market.

Another feature of monopolistic competition is that the number
of firms is assumed to be small enough so that each can know the
other's actions. This leads to the logical corollary that since a price
cut by one firm can be met quickly by similar action on the part of
the others there will be a tendency to maintain prices by tacit
agreement. When one firm sets a price and its competitors abide by it,
the situation is called one of price leadership; where several firms
tacitly agree on a price, it is called an administered rather than a
competitive price. Government regulations and taxes may also introduce market imperfections.

Modern theorists no longer find it easy to define the boundaries of
competition. From one standpoint every producer is in competition
with every other producer for the consumer's dollar. Clearly, washing-
machine manufacturers are in competition with radio and automobile
manufacturers, and also with savings banks and insurance companies,
for the consumer's surplus.[99]

The classic definitions of the market still provide the terminology
for analysis of supply and demand. If the demand for a commodity
rises rapidly with a decrease in price, or falls rapidly with an increase,
demand is said to be elastic. If, as in the case of salt, about so much
will be consumed regardless of price the demand is inelastic. The same

[99] See James S. Duesenberry, *Income, Saving, and the Theory of Consumer
Behavior* (Cambridge: Harvard University Press, 1949).

terms may also be applied to supply. Effective demand is that which operates in the market. A purchaser who will buy if the price falls to a certain point is part of the potential demand, but his demand is not effective as long as the price remains above this level.

Monetary theory links distribution and market theory to the central economic concept of value. Money is defined as a uniform medium of exchange and measure of value. It may have many forms—vegetable, animal, or mineral—so long as it acceptably performs the functions of a common denominator for comparing the worth of unlike goods or services. Being by definition the most liquid form of capital, money may also perform the function of a store of value. The demand for money for this purpose is known as liquidity preference. Changes in the value of money are measured in relation to goods in the form of price indices. Theories about what confers value upon economic products are numerous and abstract. The historian may work with economic concepts without subscribing to any one theory of value.

The study of trade, usually on an international basis, is closely related to monetary or price considerations.[100] Trade, in theory, permits an increased division of labor between different producing areas, groups, or individuals, thus permitting goods to be produced by those areas or persons whose real costs of production are least. The producer gains by being able to sell his goods in the market where the demand is greatest, the consumer by making his purchases in the market where the cost is least. International trade permits any given country to specialize in the production of those items that can be made with the greatest comparative advantage.

Goods are the visible imports and exports of international trade, but along with them come and go various services like shipping, insurance, investments, interest payments, and emigrant remittances, which are called invisible items, and also transfers of precious metals. Ideally the total value of goods plus invisible items moving in each direction should balance. In actuality a balancing item may be in the form of a bookkeeping credit or of securities, either of which may on occasion be defaulted. This balancing of claims may occur between only two nations (bilateral trade), or between the total payments due to and from many nations (multilateral trade). Thus pounds sterling earned in the United States by exporting to Great Britain

---

[100] See Donald B. Marsh, *World Trade and Investment* (New York: Harcourt, Brace and Company, 1951); and Charles P. Kindleberger, *International Economics* (Homewood, Ill.: Richard D. Irwin, 1953).

constitute foreign exchange on London and may be used to pay for imports into the United States from, say, Burma. Burmese importers may then use these pounds to purchase goods from Great Britain.

Three special areas of economic research have particular relevance for historians: business cycle analysis, economic development, and entrepreneurship. Business cycle study has proceeded on both the theoretical and the empirical or historical levels.[101] The National Bureau of Economic Research has studied the business cycle in the United States in great detail back as far as 1869. For earlier years the evidence is scanty and its reliability is often questioned.[102] Some scholars such as the late Joseph A. Schumpeter have sought to support their theoretical models historically.[103] Such studies are of particular interest in illustrating the difficulty of testing hypotheses from historical evidence.

Concentration upon economic development or growth as a special field stems partly from the studies of national income pursued at the National Bureau of Economic Research, and partly from the interest of the United States in underdeveloped areas since World War II.[104] Research has been largely empirical and historical, and has illustrated the drawing together of the social sciences. It has been found that comparative economic growth cannot be divorced from culture patterns, social structure, and entrepreneurial leadership.

Entrepreneurship had no significant place in classical theory. Business leaders were expected to adjust rationally and predictably to

[101] For a summary of theories see Gottfried Haberler, ed., *Readings in Business Cycle Theory* (Philadelphia: American Economic Association, 1944); and Gottfried Haberler, *Prosperity and Depression* (Geneva: League of Nations, 1941). For a summary of empirical findings see Wesley C. Mitchell, *What Happens During Business Cycles* (New York: National Bureau of Economic Research, 1951).

[102] See Simon Kuznets, "National Income Estimates for the United States Prior to 1870," *Journal of Economic History*, 12:115–130 (Spring 1952); Walter B. Smith and Arthur H. Cole, *Fluctuations in American Business, 1790–1860* (Cambridge: Harvard University Press, 1935); and Willard L. Thorp, *Business Annals* (New York: National Bureau of Economic Research, 1926).

[103] Joseph A. Schumpeter, *Business Cycles* (2 vols.; New York: McGraw-Hill Book Company, 1939).

[104] See Simon Kuznets, *National Income: A Summary of Findings* (New York: National Bureau of Economic Research, 1946); National Bureau of Economic Research, Universities – National Bureau Committee on Economic Research, *Problems in the Study of Economic Growth* (New York, July 1949, mimeo.); and Bert F. Hoselitz, ed., *The Progress of Underdeveloped Areas* (Chicago: University of Chicago Press, 1952).

conditions of the market. Comparative study of economic systems and the great depression of the 1930's strongly suggested that there were variable factors involved in the response of entrepreneurs. Schumpeter's *The Theory of Economic Development,* originally published in Germany in 1906, was translated into English in 1934 and became the basis for ascribing innovation and economic change to the functions of the entrepreneur. Since the late 1940's there has been considerable interdisciplinary empirical research on conditions tending to promote or retard innovating entrepreneurship.[105]

Economic progress is, of course, susceptible to many definitions, but those generally used by economists are: increase in real per capita income, or real product per worker. "Real" means money units adjusted for price changes, and "per capita" means the national total divided by the population. These concepts are somewhat abstract and not entirely satisfactory for all purposes. They do not take into account the effects of different distributions of income among various segments of the population; they cannot accurately measure goods and services that do not pass through a market; and they tend to include income produced by or spent on disutilities, such as some parts of income spent on commuting to work.

In addition to these theoretical areas of interest, economists devote much of their time to the description and analysis of concrete economic phenomena and the functioning of actual economic organizations. Often referred to as applied economics, such fields include the practical study of banking, industrial relations, management, insurance, government fiscal and monetary policy, and transportation. The other social sciences also have their "applied" fields, but applied economics provides perhaps the best example of the blending of theoretical analysis and empirical research. For this reason, as well as for the intrinsic importance of the findings, the various areas of applied economics are of interest to historians.

Conclusion

If the reader is not quite sure that he understands the meaning of many of the terms and concepts mentioned in this chapter, he is in no worse situation than other social scientists. Even leading scholars in disciplines as closely related as sociology and social psychology find

[105] See Harvard University Research Center in Entrepreneurial History, *Change and the Entrepreneur,* and its quarterly journal, *Explorations in Entrepreneurial History,* 1949–54; also William Miller, ed., *Men in Business.*

difficulty in precise communication. The aura of implication that every word carries differs with the scholar's interests and training.

In spite of difficulties in terminology and communication, the social sciences have value for the historian seeking to understand past social reality. One value, none the less important for being negative, is that knowledge of the problems of social research and theory arms him against accepting superficial social generalizations, and oversimplifying historical problems.

A positive value follows from the fact that because history is all-embracing, no historian, however brilliant, has sufficient knowledge and imagination to perceive all the facets of his material. The social sciences deal with explicit topics which the historian may explore in his research and account for in his syntheses. For example, the scholar investigating the past of cities, whether in ancient or modern times, can benefit from understanding the concepts and methods used in studies of urbanization made by other social scientists. Much of this gain from increased awareness of the elements involved should accrue regardless of the soundness of the particular concepts or hypotheses. The economist, for example, sees a market as the essential core of a city. Whether this is a valid approach or not, it warns the historian to consider such relationships. Similarly, ecologists see the essence of urban problems in a competitive struggle for the control of those elements of the environment that are needed for life or growth by individuals or groups, and again the historian may direct his attention to such matters without accepting the ideas of this school.

Another result of a social science approach is the emphasis on finding norms and types that will permit the erection of theoretical models. This inevitably leads to efforts to measure and quantify. The historian has always used some quantitative methods, but statistical and mathematical training can increase his sensitivity and skill in the use of such research tools. Proper selection of samples and tests for the significance of the statistical results derived from small numbers of cases, such as the chi square test, are extremely useful techniques for the historian.

While the term model, so dear to theoreticians, sounds imposing and perhaps overly abstract, it may actually refer to no more than two or three connected propositions, which the historian would use as a logical guide. Such advance definition of the questions to be examined is helpful in that it calls attention to the need for finding indices that will be meaningful. An index may be reliable or unreliable, exact or inexact, but it is often all the historian has to work with. Price levels, for example, may be a fairly inexact index of the swings of the business cycle, but for many centuries they have to suffice. Social scientists have been quite ingenious at finding indices for movements that are not in themselves recorded, and historians should often give the matter more thought before deciding that some trend is not measurable.

Another value of models, or propositions stated in advance—one stressed in the preceding chapter—is that they make explicit some at least of the interests and biases of the research worker. The need for awareness of bias, in turn, rests on the widely accepted psychological theory that selectivity in the individual's response to any stimulus is unavoidable. The remedy proposed by psychologists is not to strive to eliminate the element of selectivity, not to assume that by careful attention one can become an objective recording machine, but rather to define the basis for selection. If the historian can formulate his interests (or biases) in propositional or categorical terms, he can affirm with greatly increased reliability the existence or nonexistence of relevant information in the material that he examines. As Alfred Marshall, the famous economist, expressed it, "the most reckless and treacherous of all theorists is he who professes to let facts and figures speak for themselves." [106]

[106] "The Present Position of Economics (1885)" in A. C. Pigou, ed., *Memorials of Alfred Marshall* (London: Macmillan and Co., 1925), p. 168.

4 PROBLEMS OF HISTORICAL ANALYSIS

A better understanding of the problem of historical causation is one of the great values of social science study. By a more sustained analysis of the nature of historical causation historians can make a highly significant contribution to an understanding of the past and to the formulation of policies based on past experience. Interpretations of past experience are the points of reference for the formation of opinions and the making of policies. A large responsibility for providing bases for policy making lies with historians—a responsibility, moreover, that the historical profession cannot evade. The central problem of history is the analysis of change, and historians, whether they wish it or not, furnish the materials to guide or at least to justify policies, opinions, and predictions.

There are two kinds of contribution that historians can make to an understanding of human behavior. One is descriptive. In the descriptive function, events that actually took place and the order in which they occurred are identified. This function is "scientific" in the sense that it establishes credible evidence ("facts") by the critical use of documents. But if the investigator stops at this point and declines to analyze the *how* and the *why* of the temporal sequences that he describes, he is mistaking the initial task for the actual problem. The truly scientific function begins where the descriptive function stops. The scientific function involves not only identifying and describing temporal sequences; it also involves explaining them.

When we speak of explaining or understanding a given sequence of events, we mean that we undertake to give reasons for those particular events or, in other words, to explain why they occurred in that particular order. To do so is to make a statement about causation.[1] No understanding of causation can come from a mere descriptive statement of sequence. When causal relationships enter into the interpretation we have gone far beyond description; we have begun to explain.

The social sciences do not solve the problem of analyzing time sequences but they do contribute to the historian's understanding of

[1] See pp. 146–148, *infra.*

why men, groups, and societies behave in the way they do. They provide ways of looking at the evidence that research experience has shown to be helpful. The first step in the analysis of historical time sequences is not close scrutiny of "the documents," but rather an informed understanding of the factors that condition life in the world around us. If the historian cannot understand the behavior of individuals and groups in his own time and in his own culture, he is unlikely to be able to understand life in an earlier period and in a different cultural context. There are, to be sure, serious dangers involved in reading history backwards and in interpreting the past in the light of the present. But the historian's attempt to dissociate himself from contemporary conflicts and ideologies scarcely implies that he should strip himself of his priceless human experience. Nor does it imply that he should deny himself the use of the techniques that social scientists have devised for analyzing contemporary situations and events. The only argument for dissociating oneself from the present is the persistent need for objectivity.

Knowledge of the present increases our understanding of the past. Familiarity with the concepts and methods that social scientists have devised for the analysis of contemporary social processes facilitates the investigation of similar processes when encountered in the historical record. Conversely, historical knowledge of the past can illumine our understanding of the present. It serves at the same time to sharpen the tools of analysis and to extend the range of evidence that the nonhistorical social sciences use.

There is, however, one important sense in which the demands made upon the historian are greater than those made upon the specialized social scientist. Like other social scientists, the historian can break down by analytic methods the complex of factors involved in human interaction; but because he is a historian, he must also undertake to appraise larger interrelationships and attempt a general synthesis. The analysis of interrelations goes on in all social science, but the attempt to make a general synthesis of all major factors at work in a given conjuncture of events is peculiar to historical studies. It is true that monographic studies in history may isolate special segments for intensive analysis; but the conscientious historian, even when engaged upon monographic research, never permits himself to forget the final goal, namely, comprehensive synthesis. Further, the historian not only strives for an understanding of the total situation *as it is* at any given point of time, but also undertakes to explain how that situation *came to be.* From the historical point of view an event is not something isolated. It is not, as the botanist's specimen is sometimes erroneously held to be, something distinct which can be transfixed with a pin and fastened to a board with a label attached. Both are always parts of a process, the precipitates of the interplay of dynamic factors operating through preceding events and probably continuing to operate through succeeding events. The significance of each lies in its relations to a past and to a future.

Reasons such as these make it vital for the social science historian to keep himself informed about the concepts and hypotheses developed by the nonhistorical social sciences. The historian's task is of considerably greater complexity than the task facing any of the nonhistorical social sciences. The complex of factors operative in a given situation is what intrigues the historian. Historical complexities, while baffling, are not unresolvable. But if we are to understand them, the use of a wide variety of carefully chosen analytical tools is required. Given adequate tools and skill in their use, the problem is not insuperable. Factors can be identified and analyzed, even though the data do not provide adequate comprehension of all particulars. The tendencies to which the factors give rise can be evaluated, for they are not without knowable effects and direction. Interpretative synthesis is possible, and the problem is one of "discovering in the data the modes and tendencies of action and interaction." [2]

Methodology in causal analysis is still relatively crude and speculative. On the philosophical level the possibility of knowledge of causes, of prediction, and of the application of reason to the solution of social problems is still vigorously contested. The present Committee recognizes the force of the warnings in Bulletin 54. The dangers of loose thinking in the analysis of causation are certainly real and must not be minimized. Yet historians have always dealt with problems involving causation and will undoubtedly continue to do so, even though they may shun explicit use of the word "cause."

The hesitation that many historians feel about undertaking explicit causal analysis stems in part from a belief that such analyses must produce definitive results. Mathematical or mechanical conceptions of scientific analysis of causation, it is true, require exact weights for factors and insist on measured relationships. The historical context does not usually provide data of this kind, and methods of causal

[2] Ralph E. Turner, *The Great Cultural Traditions* (New York: McGraw-Hill Book Company, 1941), Vol. II, p. 1234.

analysis must necessarily be appropriate to the data. Capacity to predict effects in a sequence cannot transcend uncertainties in the evidence. Nevertheless, a scientific "law" does not state certainties, it merely states probabilities; and an appropriate statement of measured relationships always includes an estimate of probable error. When dealing with certain historical problems on which the evidence is scanty or of doubtful reliability, we may find the probable error to be so great as to invalidate *any* general statement of causal relationship. If this is the case, intellectual honesty demands that the situation be faced frankly. History has always challenged the intellectual ingenuity of mankind, but if historians were readier to admit the existence of unsolved problems, history might become even more challenging. In all science, social as well as physical, much useful theory and many fascinating explorations do not yield complete knowledge. In the analysis of causation the true scientific spirit involves the determination of the more or less, the prediction of probabilities rather than certainties, the conscientious search for techniques to overcome the limitations of the evidence, and a willingness to admit that sometimes we do not have the answers.

Concepts and Hypotheses as Analytical Tools

Every prediction and every policy designed to guide future conduct rests on causal assumptions. When we predict, we say, "If X takes place, then Y will probably follow." When we decide upon a policy, we say, "If we do A, then B will probably happen as a result." Statements of this kind are embryonic formulations of a theory, since they assert that certain relationships exist between phenomena of designated types. Similarly, when the historian has a "hunch" or an insight regarding the meaning of his evidence, he is really formulating a theory. He has in effect picked out certain segments of the data and asserted that they are related in a significant way.

In trying—as all historians do—to interpret their data and to select certain facts as significant for their analysis, historians engage in a form of mental activity very similar to that of the policy maker and the forecaster. The only type of historical research that neither implicitly nor explicitly makes use of theory is the purely narrative chronicle which simply records events without indicating inter-relationships.[3] Any other type of historical research must necessarily

[3] Even this is contested, since the process of "establishing the facts" about an event involves theory.

select those events that are recorded and those that are emphasized as significant. But if the historian selects, he does so according to some criterion. This criterion of selection is not inherent in the data; it is supplied by the historian.

Were the products of the historian's work regarded merely as entertainment, without either practical or pedagogical value, there would be no reason to choose principles of selection and interpretation. The historian could then be as arbitrary as he chose, and no one could dispute him. Similarly, no problem would exist if he were interested solely in supporting the ideology of a particular group, for then others would already have supplied him with principles. But if the historian is prepared to take responsibility for his results, if he is willing to vouch for them as valid interpretations of the past and reliable guides for the formation of future policies, then he has a duty to justify his choice of principles of selection and interpretation, to justify them not only to his own conscience but also to his professional colleagues and to all who permit his work to influence their opinions. History as social science rests on the postulate that history can be more than entertainment and more than ideology. History as social science insists that principles of selection and interpretation must be rationally chosen and rationally established; and it suggests that this can be done only by making the theories upon which it is based explicit and open to objective appraisal.

We have already discussed the nature of social science concepts and hypotheses and defined a number of social science terms. Subsequent chapters discuss various theoretical approaches at greater length and indicate both their possibilities and their limitations. At this point it must be noted that the manner in which theories are generally used in the social sciences differs slightly from the way in which they are generally employed in the natural sciences. Theories in the natural sciences are often used to sum up a great number of experimental observations by means of a generalized statement or "law." Once it was customary to refer to these theories as "laws of nature," which were immutable and eternally true, and scientific inquiry was essentially an inquiry designed to find out how these laws operated. This view of scientific inquiry and of scientific truth is now less widely held than formerly, but many natural science theories are still essentially generalizations arrived at inductively from a mass of experimental evidence.

Theories of this type could also exist in the social sciences. Indeed, whenever we slip into such phrases as "History teaches us that . . ." or "The lessons of history are . . . ," we are stating generalized inductive theories of this kind. Some "laws" of economics, such as Gresham's law and the theory of diminishing returns, may likewise be regarded as falling into this category. In social science inquiry it is more helpful to think of theories not as means of summing up a mass of data already obtained, but as means of guiding the search for data and of assisting the process of analysis and interpretation. Theories in this sense are explanatory devices. They are constructed experimentally and they are evaluated in terms of how well they enable us to discover, analyze, and explain the evidence.

Any historian, therefore, who attempts to use social science theories in his work must clearly understand that he is taking part in an experiment. These theories are not statements of eternal and immutable truth; they are, rather, statements that *may possibly provide valid explanations.* The task of the social science historian and of all other social scientists is to discover, by a process of testing and experiment, which theories are valid in whole or in part, how they relate to other theoretical formulations, and how other theories having greater validity may be constructed. The test of validity in this context is a practical one: How well does this theory *explain* the evidence? Does it help us to *understand?*

Some social scientists speak of a "theory" when referring to what the natural scientist would call a hypothesis, or rather a set of hypotheses. A theory in this sense must be distinguished from a *conception of history,* which is the historian's general view of the nature of man and of the historical process. And both theories and general conceptions must be distinguished from *concepts,* which are the raw materials of theories. A concept is a mental construction, an abstract idea that refers either to a class of phenomena or to certain aspects or characteristics that a range of phenomena have in common. Thus, a concept is an analytical and theoretical approach, a way of looking at the data. A cluster of concepts provides a means of making the subject matter intellectually manageable, for purposes of identifying different aspects, separating them, and analyzing them. The concept of economic man, for example, is a fiction, an "as if," as are legal concepts such as the corporation as a person.[4] Concepts by definition are abstractions from reality, designating types of movements, persons, behavior, or other classes of phenomena. Concepts are used for

4 See Beard, Bulletin 54, pp. 7–8, for discussion of the "as if."

organizing and analyzing; but they are also generalizing devices, containing implicit theoretical assumptions, and must be linked with explicit hypotheses if they are offered as historical explanations of particular situations.

Concepts, and therefore theories, can be developed at several different levels of abstraction. For example, we observe that in Western civilization many economic tasks are carried out by organizations of people which we refer to as business units or firms. We observe, too, that the affairs of these business units are conducted by people who have certain legal and other responsibilities for what the firm does, and who enjoy certain rights and rewards in return for their services. This general class of persons we can group together under the concept of *business executives.* A concept of this nature is sometimes referred to as a *real type.* Alternatively, we may observe that in each and every business unit certain general functions are performed: for example, somebody decides what is to be produced, in what quantity, where, and by what methods. These and other functions are often grouped together under the general name of "entrepreneurial functions" or "entrepreneurship," and the concept of the "entrepreneur" is developed to refer to the person who performs these functions. A concept of this kind is sometimes referred to as an *ideal type,* since it does not necessarily refer directly to any one particular person or group of persons. It may be possible in certain cases to identify one or a few actual individuals in a business firm who correspond closely to our concept of the entrepreneur, but in other cases it may not be. In the giant corporation of modern times, for instance, entrepreneurial functions are performed by a great variety of people, and there is no one individual who corresponds exactly to the concept. An ideal type, then, is a fiction; a real type is not a complete fiction, but a general class of real people or events. Both are concepts but they represent different levels of abstraction.[5]

While a theory may be highly abstract, hypotheses that are actually used in the process of investigation and interpretation must be phrased in terms sufficiently concrete to rule out any ambiguity as to the range of empirical phenomena to which they refer. A hypothesis so framed

[5] See Arthur Spiethoff, "Pure Theory and Economic Gestalt Theory: Ideal Types and Real Types," in Frederic C. Lane and Jelle C. Riemersma, eds., *Enterprise and Secular Change,* pp. 444–463. The sections on method in this volume merit the most careful attention. For the entrepreneur as an ideal type, see Fritz Redlich, "The Business Leader in Theory and Reality," *American Journal of Economics and Sociology,* 8:223–237 (April 1949).

is said to be an *operational working hypothesis,* and it will be found that most such hypotheses either include concepts of a relatively low degree of abstraction or else are accompanied by a set of precise definitions which make clear the empirical referent of each concept used. It is not possible, for example, to test the hypothesis that "The process of industrialization in a society is always accompanied by a shift in the social classes from which entrepreneurs are recruited," unless and until we have made clear in operational terms what is meant by the concepts of industrialization, social class, and the entrepreneur. If we neglect to do this, our hypothesis remains nothing more than a collection of vague generalities which can mean anything or nothing.

Hypotheses are propositions that assert the existence of relationships among phenomena and thus differ from concepts. As a matter of logical structure, hypotheses may be expressed either as declarative statements or as questions. For example: "If the rate of interest rises, the volume of new investment will fall." "Is a rise in the rate of interest always followed by a fall in the volume of new investment?" Such hypotheses are sometimes developed directly from study of the evidence, but they may be derived by deduction from a general theory. In the example just given, our hypothesis is derived from the general theory of prices and value. In such a case the hypothesis is *implied by* the theory; if the theory is valid, the hypothesis should be confirmed by the evidence. A test of the hypothesis is therefore a partial test of the theory.

As far as the social science historian is concerned, it will probably be most helpful if he thinks of hypotheses as questions that he asks of his data. Historians are understandably reluctant to accept as their primary task the testing of general theories which other social scientists have developed, and perhaps it is well that this should be so. For the historian the value of social science concepts and theories lies in the fact that they extend the range of questions that he can put to his data, and at the same time provide some indication of the kinds of data required if his questions are to be answered.

The more the historian is concerned with interpretations, with interrelations of all kinds, including causal interrelations, the greater is his need for an understanding of the social sciences. But social science approaches to history can never be applied mechanically. To talk glibly of developing concepts and testing hypotheses is simple; but rules of procedure of this kind will no more produce competent historians than an elementary handbook on chess can produce a Capablanca. The richer the intellectual and cultural equipment of the historian, the richer and more illuminating the results of his research will be. The use of social science approaches in historical research is merely a means, and only one, through which the historian can attempt to apply his intellectual faculties to better advantage.

Historians in the United States have become increasingly familiar with the use of conceptualized approaches. As a consequence, they have been driven to re-examine the nature and function of historical knowledge. Despite apprehensions, observes a member of the former Committee on Historiography, "the use of social science generalizations by the historian is increasing." More frequently, he notes, historians are setting themselves the task of discovering single cases that illustrate a social science generalization, and single cases that contradict it; and he comments on the appearance of numerous comparative studies designed to test the application of a social science generalization to similar sequences or trends.[6] *The steady growth of historical analyses by means of concepts and hypotheses illustrates the extent to which history has already developed as a social science.* Further development depends upon a twofold expansion: an increasing use of concepts from allied fields,[7] and greater exploitation of those ways of conceptualizing already employed and refined by historians.

Historians themselves have invented and given currency to many indispensable concepts. They have, for example, developed important analytical approaches associated with the concept of nationalism. They have developed and explored the concept of historical types, such as the Russian peasant, the Renaissance humanist, the benevolent despot, and the bourgeoisie. Important in Frederick Jackson Turner's approach was the concept of the pioneer farmer; and indeed Turner conceived of a succession of frontier types. Many general terms which have become a part of everyday speech are abstract concepts that historians employ as a way of ordering and viewing a particular context of historical circumstances, for example, imperialism, capitalism, feudalism, class conflict, revolution, democracy, the public interest, and vested rights. The concept of sea power and its correlative, command of the sea, were derived by historical study of concrete instances. The concept of balance of power is really a complex of concepts with

[6] Louis Gottschalk, *Understanding History* (New York: Alfred A. Knopf, 1950), p. 252.

[7] Cf. pp. 16, 18 ff., 32–33, 35 ff., *supra.*

a wide assortment of correlative hypotheses. Historians in the main, and students of diplomacy using historical methods, have clarified the distinctions within these concepts and have evaluated their changing temporal relevance. Revolution as a concept of one type of social movement has permitted classification of different stages in revolutions and different motives and types of revolution. One need only compare ancient Greek ideas of domestic turbulence with the modern analysis of revolution to observe the utility of well-formulated concepts.

Because of their particular concern with time sequences, historians have resorted to numerous temporal concepts, such as an event, a movement, or a period. In many instances a term for a movement, an era, or a century, although originally intended purely as a descriptive label, acquires the status of a concept—for example, "the eighteenth century," "the romantic movement," "the last frontier." Such temporal concepts are less common in other social sciences; but to the historian they are a way of dividing an essentially continuous sequence of events, for purposes of analysis. The historian's concept of a *continuum* is in fact a concept of major importance. A continuum in history is not literally "that which is absolutely continuous and selfsame." Rather, it is a set of phenomena with a fundamental common character continuing in time and space. *The historian seeks to discover and explain change; but change can be perceived and measured only by analysis of continuities and discontinuities.*

The historian employs concepts and hypotheses because of the general assumption that underlies all social science: *History is not exclusively chaos or chance: a degree of observable order and pattern, of partially predictable regularity, exists in human behavior.*

STRUCTURE AND PROCESS

Historians who have made social science part of their thinking are not satisfied to regard history only in terms of events. There are two other ways of viewing and interpreting the subject matter of history. One is in terms of the *structure* of the situation in which events take place. A business firm, a political party, a revolution, a university, a casual meeting of two acquaintances—all these may be described correctly as systems of human interaction, characterized by a greater or lesser degree of organization. The degree and mode of organization in a situation is its *structure*. The concept of structure enables us to build a theoretical bridge between the unique individual, with all his particularities and idiosyncrasies, and the environment in which the individual acts. Individual behavior and the structure of the social environment are viewed not as independent, but as interdependent. Human beings exist as parts of social organizations, and their behavior is patterned by the roles they play in those organizations and by controls enforced through a multitude of power-wielding groups, who in turn are responsive to well-established cultural traditions. An adequate explanation of a particular segment of human behavior (such as the career of a statesman) must therefore take account of the structure of the situation in which this behavior takes place. It is this structure that channels behavior into particular lines, limiting freedom of action in some directions, opening up wider possibilities in others.

Equally useful, and in the same sense scientific, is the approach to historical events in terms of *process*. Changes in a structure are frequently not random or haphazard, but follow definite patterns through time. For example, economists and other social scientists speak of "the process of industrialization." They mean that the changes that occur in a society when it moves from a predominantly agricultural to a predominantly industrial state follow a recognizable course which can be identified and analyzed *as a separable phenomenon*. Structure and process are closely related concepts, since the changes that are identified as constituting a process are always changes in a structure. They reflect the interaction of the parts of that structure. The process of industrialization, for example, consists in a complex series of changes in the size and composition of the labor force, the techniques and organization of production, the relationships of capital and labor, and many other factors. By calling it a process we refer to the fact that these changes follow a pattern which can be described and analyzed.

The related concepts of structure and process provide a highly useful guiding thread in the analysis of causation. They are fundamental to any systematic study of change. They enable the historian to penetrate beneath the superficial manifestations of change and to seek an explanation in terms of underlying trends and conditioning factors. For example, to analyze the history of the American family,[8] one needs to study its internal structure (the interrelated roles of father, son, daughter, mother, uncle, and other kin), its relationship to the culture and society of which it is a part (the effects of industrialism, urban living, wider educational opportunities, the "emancipation" of women, and similar elements), and the processes through which

8 See p. 46n, *supra.*

changes in internal structure are affected by, and in turn affect, its external relationships.[9] Or again, one would analyze the outbreak of World War I not so much in terms of assassinations and ultimatums as in terms of the social (especially the political and economic) structures of the national states involved, the structure of international relations (perhaps with particular emphasis on international trade and investment and the struggle for markets and raw materials), and the process by which conflicts arising from internal strains in the structures of national states were reflected in and aggravated by conflicts in the international sphere.

An approach that uses the concepts of structure and process, in short, leads us to ask questions that cannot be answered merely by identifying the succession of events. Events are of the moment, episodic; process and structure have duration in time, recognizable patterns, and a high degree of continuity. An approach that focuses on underlying trends and movements makes it possible to see particular events and the actions of particular men in a larger, more revealing perspective.[10]

Approach to the History of Culture

Investigation of structure and process is especially suggestive in studying the history of cultures. A central aspect of a culture is the social process of learning. By intercommunication within a culture, knowledge, ideas, and organized patterns of behavior are transmitted to succeeding generations. By contacts between different cultures, new elements are diffused and are combined in new orientations of the cultures. The study of structure and process on the high level of general cultural history is perhaps the most challenging and rewarding task suggested to historians by other social science disciplines.

The history of long-range changes in a culture is a kind of contemplative and abstract history. It requires a higher level of abstraction than either economic or political history. The historian of culture looks at long-range tendencies, at potentials of a culture, and the degree to which potentials are realized. This demands more generalized concepts and more abstract hypotheses than is the case with generalizations

9 For an example of this type of analysis see Marion J. Levy, Jr., *The Family Revolution in Modern China* (Cambridge: Harvard University Press, 1949).

10 For this discussion of structure and process, and for the balance of this chapter, the Committee owes much to Ralph E. Turner and to the last chapter of his *Great Cultural Traditions*, Vol. II. On the concept of process, see also R. M. MacIver, *Social Causation* (Boston: Ginn and Company, 1942), pp. 126–135.

about concrete events or about causal factors in short-range sequences. Explanation of dynamic potentials in a culture, or of the structural characteristics which make certain cultures relatively static or given to slow change, is nevertheless a form of causal analysis, even though the causal hypotheses involved are far removed by abstraction from concrete factors in a situation. Needless to say, the data from which the cultural historian infers the existence and characteristics of a culture are as real and concrete as any used in political or economic history; but they are selected with a different interest in view and used as evidence for generalizations at a different level. A historian who attempts to assess the potentials, dynamics, and limitations of a culture seeks to appraise the whole, much as de Tocqueville did in his highly contemplative but eminently valid assessment of *Democracy in America*. To use the popular idiom, de Tocqueville was trying to explain "what made America tick." This is in a sense the basic question for the historian of a culture.

Analysis of the interplay of cultural factors in the context of history is no easy task. Human beings in every time and place are largely unconscious of the conditioning effect of their cultural traditions; and the documents and other artifacts they leave do not give the historian self-evident explanations of the influence of the culture on individual actions. But it is not impossible for the historian (and the cultural anthropologist) to achieve some understanding of what seems to people in a particular time and place to be normal and natural, i.e. what they take for granted. He can often observe better than the historical actors in the situation the peculiarities of their culture as contrasted with others. He can develop the implicit from the explicit. He can separate for analysis parts of the cultural tradition, for example, practical skills and factual knowledge (technological); the institutional tradition (organizational); and intellectual and emotional orientation (ideational). These may all be viewed as structures with recognizable patterns; and their processes of change may be identified and analyzed. They are interconnected, and the interplay in the relations between them constitutes a basic problem for historical research.

One convenient way of analyzing the interplay of the parts of a culture is in terms of the groups of persons who transmit or diffuse the bodies of knowledge and tradition. Particular groups (priestly, military, commercial) that play an active part in transmitting important skills, learning, or traditions are said to serve as *carriers* of the culture.

When Dixon Ryan Fox wrote of "Culture in Knapsacks," [11] he was dealing with the carriers of culture from the eastern seaboard of the United States to the frontier. Since the carriers of culture are men, they may be studied as groups and individuals. Culture is pluralistic; there is no universal man who carries the whole culture. A psychological concept, the human tendency toward highly selective perception, may be serviceable here. Individuals or groups carry and diffuse those elements of the cultural tradition that are rooted in their own experience and meaningful in terms of their particular intellectual and emotional orientation. Thus each group and each individual carries only part of the culture. In particular, it is that part of the whole culture that provides the occupational learning, sets the norms, and sanctions the interests of the group or groups with which the individual is chiefly identified. A good example of the analysis of the carrying of a part of Western culture is Hayes' study of nationalism, specifically the gradual transmission of its intellectual and emotional orientation downward, in vertical diffusion from higher social groups to lower ones.[12]

But men make traditions as well as carry them. Traditions are at once forms of social learning and group interpretations of past experience. New factual knowledge, acquired by diffusion or by discovery and invention, permits a new interpretation of the cultural tradition, for example, the development of a new form of social organization; and eventually this modification, too, becomes an accepted part of the interpretation of past experience. Thus culture grows and changes usually by small increments, as inherited traditions and ways of acting are continually modified by the necessity of meeting new problems. Typically this cumulative reinterpretation and reshaping of the cultural tradition takes place covertly and without any conscious awareness of the direction of change; but there are occasions when people pause and take stock, as it were, perhaps at a time of crisis when the adequacy of the accepted cultural tradition in providing an effective solution to an urgent problem is put to the test.

There are, therefore, discontinuities as well as continuities in cul-

[11] Dixon Ryan Fox, *Ideas in Motion* (New York: D. Appleton-Century Company, 1935).

[12] Carlton J. H. Hayes, *Essays on Nationalism* (New York: Macmillan Company, 1928), pp. 69–80; *The Historical Evolution of Modern Nationalism* (New York: Macmillan Company, 1950).

tural change. There are times of cultural disorganization and even cultural crisis, when elements of the inherited tradition, such as basic patterns of behavior, work routines, and emotional and intellectual attitudes, are seriously disrupted and the culture seems to lose much of its internal cohesion. Ordinarily such discontinuities are followed by the emergence of new cultural patterns and new interpretations of the cultural tradition. In the depression of the 1930's the widespread disruption of traditional ways of acting and thinking in the United States—the feeling of being lost in a world from which the old familiar landmarks had disappeared—was a symptom of partial cultural disorganization. And in some but not all respects one might cite the New Deal to illustrate cultural emergence. In dealing with periods of rapid cultural change of this type, it is important to inquire to what extent the existing cultural tradition provided an adequate and effective solution to immediate problems; the emergence of cultural change, of a redefinition of the cultural tradition and of its potentialities, indicates a discrepancy between the problem and its traditional solution. It is in this context that consideration of the "vitality" and "creativity" of cultures becomes relevant.

THE PROBLEM OF CONVERGENT APPROACHES

There is for many scholars a certain insidious attraction in the writing of general histories of cultures. Certainly it is possible in this field to attain a high level of analysis and to develop hypotheses of profound significance. However, the suspicion is perhaps not altogether unjustified that certain attempts to write general histories of cultures, with their high order of abstraction and the consequent difficulty of proving or disproving hypotheses by reference to any particular set of facts, reflect not so much a desire to reach conclusions of scientific validity as a disinclination to undertake the arduous task of utilizing social science approaches on a lower level, where sense and nonsense can more easily be distinguished. If this variety of historical research were the only one in which such approaches could be applied, a certain skepticism as to their utility would be justified.

Social science approaches, however, can be utilized on several levels. The problem is essentially that of deciding on what level of abstraction one wishes to provide an explanation. The historian's primary data consist of testimony about particular events and particular facts, and he is traditionally interested in the concrete and the individual. Certain types of questions cannot be answered on this level. How far we choose to go in abstracting from these particular phenomena and in developing generalized concepts and hypotheses depends entirely on the nature of the problems we set ourselves. At one extreme the historian may work on the highly abstract level of general cultural change; on the other, on the level of the particular and the unique. The more general the problem, the more abstract, in most cases, must be his concepts and hypotheses.

The problem of convergent approaches is the problem of showing how explanations given at one level of analysis can be generalized and synthesized at higher levels. The most general level of all is that of the history of culture; but between this and explanations of particular events there should be a continuous ladder of increasingly general syntheses. Similarly, there is a considerable difference in levels of abstraction between the general theory of relativity and the observation that apples fall from trees; but we may be sure that if there could not be derived from the general theory of relativity an adequate explanation of the behavior of apples falling from trees, this general theory would not stand much chance of being accepted by physicists. This is the nature of scientific explanation. The task facing historians is essentially of the same order: it is that of insuring that the explanations they provide of general cultural change on the one hand and of particular historical events on the other are logically consistent, and of bringing to bear upon the explanation of particular events concepts and hypotheses that are valid in terms of a more general theory.

A CONVERGENT APPROACH

Historians of different temperaments and training will prefer different ways of combining and varying social science concepts in the analysis of particular problems; and an experimental attitude—a willingness to put different approaches to the test—is of course to be encouraged. One way of tackling the problem may be suggested here, purely as an illustration. A strictly scientific treatment would start with the identification of a problem. Most historians, however, like to focus on concrete events and to proceed by narrative exposition; they are likely therefore to begin with the dramatic context—the situation, the persons, the location in space and time. As a method of presentation in contradistinction to a method of analysis, this has much to recommend it. Nevertheless, since the concepts and hypotheses to be used depend upon careful formulation of the problem, the historian will contrive to define his problem and indicate how he intends to handle it in the initial setting of the historical stage.

Since the historian is dealing with the behavior of human beings in a social context, he will then proceed (we refer now to his order of analysis rather than to his method of presentation) to analyze the structure of the various situations in which his *dramatis personae* find themselves. What social roles do they play? What systems of sanctions do they encounter in playing these roles, what groups or individuals exert these sanctions, and how effectively are they enforced? Do we find conflict and inconsistency between patterns of sanctions or between those patterns and the predispositions of the actors? Are there processes of change at work? If so, is the behavior of the persons being studied consistent with these long-term tendencies? These and many other more specific questions will at once suggest themselves. In fact, any historian who has grasped the concept of social structure will find examples awaiting analysis at every turn: groups, individuals in groups, groups as functioning parts of society, demographic aspects of groups, their position with respect to possession of goods or wealth, their attendant position of power in economic relations, their political influence, their position in respect to command of the means of violence, and their position in respect to ideas and the manipulation of symbols. For analysis of group action, particularly in the political sphere, the historian may find Lasswell's categories suggestive, especially manipulation of symbols, control of goods, and control of the means of violence.[13]

The historian who is concerned with social change in the broadest sense, and in particular with the role of ideas, may find helpful certain approaches that can be derived from anthropology and the sociology of knowledge. Analyses focused on the roles that particular men and groups play in generating and diffusing new knowledge and other cultural elements serve to correct the inadequacy of an abstract linear treatment of an idea as it changes through time. Ideas have functions for the groups that hold them; an adequate explanation of the history of an idea must include some analysis of the functions that this idea performed for different groups. A linear treatment of an idea, on

[13] Harold D. Lasswell, *Politics* (New York: Whittlesey House, 1936); see also Harold D. Lasswell and Abraham Kaplan, *Power and Society* (New Haven: Yale University Press, 1950) for propositions concerning influence, power, symbols, and practices.

the other hand, tends to emphasize its development in terms of its own inner logic, and thus to slight its meaning in particular contexts.

Analysis of the changing function of ideas in time and space places intellectual development in its social setting and can attempt to show the role of ideas in cultural change. For example, historians have frequently observed how a new idea opens up possibilities of change in a culture that were not perceived and perhaps not present before. A case in point is the early development of modern science, which was inspired by the idea that natural phenomena were not unpredictable, reflecting the haphazard operations of some supernatural agency, but followed "laws" that could be discovered by the exercise of reason.[14] Such a cultural accretion opens up new potentialities for growth; it extends the limits of the possible. This concept of the *potentiality* of a culture at different points of time clearly needs more refinement and critical examination than it has yet received, but it may nevertheless be useful. When observing a culture that seems stagnant, for example, or one which is changing very slowly, a historian might well investigate the factors—physical, social, and cultural—that set limits to the possible range of alternative directions of growth. Balancing this concept of potentiality, then, we have the concept of *options* or alternatives; and both these concepts rest upon the concept of a culture as a *state of knowledge. The state of knowledge at a given time, when analyzed, may reveal the limits of the possible; that is, that some of the supposed options were not real options, or that the supposed options fell short of the potentialities that in fact existed.*

It is important that the historian, in using the concepts of culture and social structure, should not implicitly assume a greater degree of homogeneity than is actually present. To reify a culture or a social structure, as some writers have abstracted the state, to regard it as something that can exist independently and apart from the behavior of its individual members, would be to fall into the fallacy of misplaced concreteness. Even a tightly integrated society, indeed a totalitarian one, exhibits a measure of plurality. All groups participate in the transmission and interpretation of culture, but their participation is partial, and occurs at different levels and with different degrees of intensity. Each group in pursuing its interests sees a future, judges potentialities, estimates the limits of the possible, and asks, "What can be done?"

14 See especially H. Butterfield, *The Origins of Modern Science* (New York: Macmillan Company, 1951); and Edgar Zilsel, "The Sociological Roots of Science," *American Journal of Sociology,* 47:544–562 (January 1942).

Even when a group regards its interests as identical with those of the larger society of which it forms a part, its judgment of potentialities and options is likely to be highly autistic. What it sees will depend on where it stands. A social evil, for example, may go unrecognized or be accepted as inevitable for generations, until some influential group, in the light of new knowledge or a reinterpretation of its interests, decides that it is to be defined as an evil and that something can be done about it. *Potentialities arise from the introduction of new knowledge, particularly factual knowledge, and therewith new experiences and new moral ideas; but the movement to realize a potential may have to wait for a long period until changes in group relations permit positive action.*

Judgments by groups as to what can be done provide historians with documents from which they can infer the various alternatives that different segments of a society take to be real choices. These options may not have been real alternatives, and it is proper to raise the question which were realistic appraisals of the possible and which were not. Even though subjectively held and possibly unrealistic, these group appraisals of potentiality are objective data in the historical context and provide the historian with some of his most useful evidence, particularly in regard to the process by which competing groups in society achieve and retain positions of dominance. Competing groups appeal to those parts of the cultural tradition that best rationalize their interests and best sanction their judgment of potentiality. This competition injects into the historical record an appearance of multiple choice; and the process by which competition and conflict is worked out so that finally one and only one choice is made presents the historian with classic problems of multiple causation.

Thus, in the approach suggested by concepts used in other social sciences, the historian is concerned with finding a valid explanation of particular sequences of events; he develops this explanation by relating the concrete sequence to underlying tendencies and processes of change in the structure of the society and culture. He starts with the unique historical situation and, while setting his stage, states his problem. He then analyzes the structure of the situation at several different but related levels—the immediate context, the groups involved, the structure of the society, and the cultural tradition—with particular emphasis on the processes and potentialities of change at each of these levels and how they influenced individual behavior. His conclusion, if his analysis is successful, is a generalized statement of the nature and meaning of the sequence of events in this particular culture, and an *explanation* of the sequence in terms of the causal influences affecting it. On the monographic level, a general synthesis of this variety is not necessarily called for. Research would be in order on any particular segment of the causal nexus and on any particular level of analysis.

5 CHANGE AND HISTORY

CHANGE AND THE HISTORIAN

The basic assumption of the present report is that an essential problem of history is the description and explanation of human activity through time. If the validity of this proposition is conceded, it follows that a chief task of the historian is to ascertain what has happened, to identify events in sequence, to analyze interrelationships among those events, and to discover how and why they occurred in a given order.

This is an exacting and enormous undertaking—by far the most inclusive that confronts any of the social sciences. Those of little courage may turn from it with a shudder of despair. They will argue that the historian cannot possibly attain a competence that will permit him to treat exhaustively all those aspects of human experience that are the special provinces of his fellow social scientists. They will maintain that any attempt to achieve the intellectual status of a universal man in this age of specialization is anachronistic, if not absurd. They may, indeed, contend that a description and analysis of the great complexity of human relationships through time is a phantasmagoria. Or, if they avoid this position of sheer defeatism, they may take easy refuge in mere narrative history which, even if entertaining, does little toward building a body of scientific knowledge about human behavior.

If history as a scientific study is to fulfill its high promise, it cannot be left to defeatists or narrators; and, fortunately, the task of the individual historian is not so appallingly difficult as that which confronts the collectivity of historians. Obviously the individual historian cannot describe and analyze *all* human experience through *all* time. He needs only to be aware that his own research should *contribute* to that description and analysis. Nevertheless, as he proceeds, he requires criteria to guide him both in the selection of problems for investigation and in the development of valid concepts and analytical methods. In these respects, except in regard to the authenticity of evidence, traditional history provides little aid.

It is at this point that the historian can turn with profit to the other social sciences. His first reaction may well be that these disciplines only have fancy names and abstruse language for matters that are commonplace to the historical scholar; or he may feel uncritical enchantment over learning names for things that he has handled all his professional life, much as Molière's M. Jordain in the *Bourgeois Gentilhomme* went into ecstasy when he learned that certain letters that he had pronounced since infancy were called vowels. If a reasonable balance between such extremes can be achieved, the historian is likely to find that the other social sciences can assist him in many ways. They can point out the topics to which they devote their attention because these constitute a large portion of human activity; many of them, like the institution of the family, have received almost no treatment by historians. They can suggest interrelationships among various aspects of human behavior and among events. And they can make available to the historian methods which have been developed to make observation and analysis more accurate and which may be acquired to the extent necessary for historical work more easily than one might at first imagine. In brief, a knowledge of other social sciences will help the historian to ask more pertinent questions of his data and to avoid making hasty, oversimple, and even erroneous explanations of human activity.

As we have seen, social scientists employ concepts that permit the organization of data relevant to major aspects of human behavior. These concepts are helpful in making systematic descriptions of a society—its culture, institutions, structure, physical environment, biological composition, and foci of authority—and in explaining the relationships and interactions of the parts of this society.

If this procedure is followed with reference to any moment of time, the society will appear to be in a state of rest.[1] When it is pursued through time, the society will be seen to be changing in some respects. Studies of a society at rest tend to be largely descriptive. Studies of a society through time, on the other hand, must undertake to explain the processes and patterns of change, and the forces which lead to change.

To historians, therefore, change is of particular moment, for they study the totality of human activity through time and hence encounter more change in their data than do other social scientists who

---

[1] Some would say that the society is in "equilibrium." This term is misleading because it implies a balancing of elements and a degree of harmony, and should be avoided. The same objection applies to a series of descriptions of the same society at different periods of time or many "equilibria" and to the concept of a "moving equilibrium," a method for study of changes at different points in a series.

limit the temporal scope of their observations.[2] Historians are concerned with changes in culture, institutions, social structure, foci of power, leaders, physical environment, the composition of the population, and the identifiable interconnections among such changes. They endeavor to describe changes in each of these realms, to explain how a change in one affects the others, and to analyze the new directions in which society moves. In brief, they attempt to evaluate the rate, volume, and direction of change.

CONCEPTIONS AND MISCONCEPTIONS

As the historian approaches the study of change, he finds a considerable body of general ideas regarding the subject. First, there is the obvious fact that a society is always changing to some degree, even if the change is limited to renewal of its members as a result of births and deaths. Hence, change may be said to be immanent. Second, problems of change, either its prevention or encouragement, constitute the major concern of human kind. Consequently, change is the object of most private and public policy—of attempts by man to control and regulate what takes place.

These elementary concepts may be readily accepted by the historian. When it comes to the explanation of why and how change takes place, however, the scientist encounters more serious difficulties. Here he finds many theories to entice him. If he has studied Arnold J. Toynbee's *A Study of History* (1934–39), he may have been impressed by that author's concepts of "challenge and response" and of "withdrawal and return." Or he may have come under the spell of Oswald Spengler's *The Decline of the West* (1926–28) and feel drawn to that author's comparison of society to an organism—a thing that is born, has a vigorous youth, matures, grows old, and finally dies. Or he may have been impressed with the Marxian analysis and seek to explain change primarily in terms of the struggle between socioeconomic classes and of the labor theory of value. Or he may have obtained from Montesquieu, Buckle, or Huntington a belief that the source of change is to be found in alterations in geographic and climatic conditions. Or from the social evolutionists, like Herbert Spencer,[3] he may have

---

[2] Indeed, the historian runs the risk of exaggerating change by concentrating his attention on periods of profound and rapid alterations, and largely ignoring long periods when society was relatively static and its various institutions remarkably stable.

[3] See C. de S. de Montesquieu, *De l'esprit des lois* (Geneva: Barrillot, 1748); Henry

formed an opinion that change takes place through struggles in which the "fittest" of social institutions and cultures survive. Or from some theological system he may have acquired faith in a supernatural power which determines change upon this earth.

In general, these and other grand-scale explanations of change, suggestive as they may be, are not to be evaluated by the criteria required for empirical analysis. Toynbee's generalizations, for example, must be elaborated to be testable propositions—an elaboration that the author does not provide. The concept of "challenge and response" implies that beings in society react to stimuli (a very elementary proposition of psychology), but it does not explain what stimuli under what conditions have usually resulted in a certain kind of response. Nor does the concept of "withdrawal and return" say more than that a society may attain a cultural position, subsequently lose that position, and then attain a new position of prominence. Such a descriptive statement provides no clues as to why or under what conditions a society attains or loses prominence.

Nor does Spengler's analogy provide a useful tool of analysis, for societies, although composed of human organisms, are not themselves organisms and do not behave like them. Observed and recorded data concerning societies do not indicate that changes recur within regular periods or follow the same pattern as those among animals.[4] This fact appears to eliminate from serious consideration any simple deterministic cyclical theory of change in societies over long periods of time. Yet it does not rule out cyclical movements and the possibility of discovering generalized regularities in the multiplicity of factors that affect human behavior.

The Marxist interpretation of change as a result of class conflict lacks validity because of its limited purview of operative forces and the factual fallacy in the labor theory of value, that is, that labor is the sole source of value. Rigid theories of social evolution, too, have little usefulness because observed data do not confirm their fundamental and optimistic premise of the survival of the best, nor their corollary that progress is represented by an ascending straight line, and because the definition of the best as that which survives is clearly

---

T. Buckle, *History of Civilization in England* (2 vols.; London: J. W. Parker and Son, 1857–61); Ellsworth Huntington, *Mainsprings of Civilization* (New York: John Wiley & Sons, 1945); and Herbert Spencer, *The Man versus the State* (London: Williams & Norgate, 1884).

[4] Beard, Bulletin 54, p. 6.

arbitrary and sterile. Nor does reliance upon supernatural power have relevance to scientific study for the obvious reason that by its nature neither the power nor its actions can be observed.

Apparently any generalized statement concerning change that can be scientifically useful in providing understanding of the forces at work in society and of regularities in human behavior must be as all-embracing as a description of society itself. Both logic and available evidence indicate that change can come from alterations in any one of the many aspects of a given society or from transformations in any combination of these aspects. Consequently the historian should approach his task of explaining change with a critical attitude toward grandiose concepts and monocausal systems.

In contrast to such highly generalized theories, the social sciences do not provide explanations that will fit all cases, but rather *a set of tools of analysis designed to make the study of historical change manageable.* These tools can be used by the historian without necessarily committing him to any particular kind of explanation. In the first place, it may be useful for him to consider the society that he is investigating as a *structure of relationships and interactions,* characterized by *processes of change,* and shaped by the play of many interdependent variables of a physical, social, economic, political, and intellectual nature. Second, it may be helpful if he recognizes that some of these elements are more *constant* and *stable* than others, for obviously such things as climate and geography are less subject to sudden alterations than forms of government or the techniques of production. Third, it may be of assistance to classify those types of change that originate within one of the elements mentioned above, irrespective of their effect on other elements, as *autonomous change,* and adjustments that take place in other elements in response to autonomous change as *adaptive change.*[5] Fourth, it may be profitable to distinguish between those factors of change that are inherent in a social body, like births and deaths, which may be called the *immanent factors* of change, and those outside it, like the weather and topography, which may be called the *external factors.*[6]

[5] For example, the invention of the steam engine may be regarded as autonomous change within the area of mechanical engineering, and may be studied as such; but it may also be considered from a more general point of view as having resulted from the need for greater power resources to meet the demand of European domestic and overseas markets for goods, and hence as an example of adaptive change.

[6] P. A. Sorokin stresses this last point in *Social and Cultural Dynamics* (New York: American Book Co., 1941), Vol. IV. Change resulting from the working of

Classification of the different types of factors of change does not solve the problem of historical causation, but it does provide a conceptual framework within which this problem can be handled.[7] Once again it is necessary to stress that a simple narrative or chronological description of events cannot provide an adequate analysis of causal relationships and may indeed be highly deceptive. Temporal sequence is no certain indication of the existence of a causal relationship. The problem is that of identifying logical rather than merely temporal patterns. In approaching this problem the distinction between *necessary* and *sufficient* causes is of fundamental importance.

FACTORS OF CHANGE: A GENERAL STATEMENT

In presenting their interpretation of a given event, such as the outbreak of hostilities in the American Civil War, members of the historical guild generally recognize that there was both a necessary cause (let us say, the firing on Fort Sumter) and also certain other relevant conditions which, along with the necessary cause, constituted the sufficient causes. They express this recognition by endeavoring to establish the "setting" or "background" of the subject under discussion, and then isolating what they call the "immediate" causes of change. In essence this procedure is both logically and practically sound. As ordinarily performed, however, it is highly empirical and void of the use of general concepts which would encourage systematic treatment, add to clarity, and assure adequate coverage of relevant factors. Here the historian undoubtedly can profit from the findings of other social sciences.

From the literature of economics and sociology the historian can find that, in analyzing why a certain set of changes took place, it is helpful to inquire into *the range of opportunities for alternative decisions* open to the members of the society in question and the factors that set the limits of this range. From this starting point, we are led at once to ask whether the culture, institutions, group relationships, power of leaders, and physical environment were such that the

---

factors in society he calls "immanent change," and that resulting from factors outside the society, "external change." The distinction is useful for clarification and for identifying the *origins* of change, but it should not be pushed too far. Any social change, whatever its origin, must manifest itself in processes of interaction *within* the society; and these processes, rather than the origin, are often of primary interest to the historian.

[7] See Bulletin 54, especially pp. 110–115.

members of the society could with relative freedom make one of several choices regarding private and public policy. For example, this approach would lead the historian of the pre-Civil War period to inquire how large the range of opportunities was in the Southern states for an alteration of policies concerning slavery within a span of time that could have forestalled the development of an intransigent position (if there was such a development) in the North and South. Or it might lead the historian to ask how large the range of opportunities in the North or South was with respect to actual recourse to war after the act of secession and the firing on Fort Sumter, and whether people at the time were fully aware of the range of alternatives open to them. This procedure would direct attention to investigation of the factors that limited and therefore influenced policy formation, the extent to which the relevant cultural patterns and social institutions actually were deeply ingrained, basic sources of changes, and areas of conflict.

If the subject were the industrial revolution in the eighteenth and early nineteenth centuries, a similar analysis of the range of opportunities for the use of human and material resources would probably lead to better understanding of a highly complex process. Did the English businessman have a wider range of opportunities for the mechanization of industry than the French? Was the effective demand for certain goods so much greater in England than across the Channel that it encouraged producers to adopt new methods for increasing their output? Were raw materials cheaper or more easily available? Was venture capital in greater supply? Was the labor force more adaptable to mechanized processes? Did tastes and consumption preferences differ in the two countries? Were the crucial inventions the outcome of more intensive experimentation, knowledge of mechanics, or pressure for goods than in other countries? Was the culture such that innovations and new patterns of behavior were more readily accepted than elsewhere? Was there a greater desire for gain on the part of the English entrepreneur than on that of the French, and if so, why? Answers to these and similar questions pertinent to the range of opportunities would throw light not only on the process of industrial growth but also on the reasons for the very distinctive combination of advantages in England.

These illustrations suggest that the concept of the range of opportunities for alternative decisions may well be a highly useful tool in the study of change through time. They also indicate that this range depends on many cultural and social conditions, for example, on the *degree of rigidity* in the society in question. If a society's culture, institutions, groups, ideologies, and leadership are highly patterned or structured (that is, rigidly set in conventional and traditional patterns), change will take place more slowly and with greater difficulty than in a society characterized by greater flexibility. This concept would lead the historian of the pre-Civil War period to inquire into the degree of rigidity in Southern culture regarding slavery and the economy which was based on slavery. Was the institution of slavery deeply ingrained? And if so, in what regions and in what classes? Were these regions and classes in well-established positions of leadership and power? Was the antislavery ideology in the North highly patterned and deep-set? Was it strong among those groups and leaders who occupied positions of power? If so, what functions did it serve for them? Where was the greatest flexibility regarding slavery, and what conditions gave rise to this flexibility?

Similar questions may be asked concerning the industrial revolution in England in the eighteenth century. Here we find much greater rigidity in the organization of the well-established and time-honored industries like woolen textiles than in the new and rapidly expanding industries like cotton manufactures. Mechanization and the use of power from inorganic sources were introduced much more rapidly in the latter than in the former. Furthermore, rigidities in attitudes and behavior were found among those who were not immediately affected by mechanization (for example, housewives who wove or spun as a spare-time activity), while the new generation of industrial entrepreneurs showed considerable flexibility. In the history of industrialization it is clear that rigidity in business methods and production techniques was a retarding factor in French economic development, whereas the absence of such rigidities was an important factor in American economic growth.[8] Similar rigidities in social structure are, of course, apparent in many of the so-called underdeveloped countries of today.[9]

Rigidity will depend in part on *the extent to which a proposed*

[8] See Charles Ballot, *L'Introduction du machinisme dans l'industrie francaise* (Lille: O. Marquant, 1923); Shepard B. Clough, *The American Way: The Economic Basis of Our Civilization* (New York: Thomas Y. Crowell Company, 1953); John E. Sawyer, "Social Structure and Economic Progress," *American Economic Review*, 41(suppl.):321–329 (May 1951); David S. Landes, "French Entrepreneurship and Industrial Growth in the Nineteenth Century," *Journal of Economic History*, 9: 45–61 (May 1949).

[9] See Bert F. Hoselitz, ed., *The Progress of Underdeveloped Areas* (Chicago: University of Chicago Press, 1952), *passim*.

change affects favorably or unfavorably the status of those segments of
society that possess influence, authority, and power, and the position of
leaders. This proposition represents a drastic modification of the
traditional belief that underprivileged segments of society have been
the breeding ground of change. Underprivileged groups have seldom
independently effected change until they or their leaders have acquired
a position of power and authority. Indeed, privileged groups are
responsible for a large measure of change, for they have the means
for initiating new undertakings and their positions free them to some
extent from tradition. Their economic resources make it easier for
them to develop and introduce innovations, while their prestige and
authority facilitate the winning of mass approval and consent. In the
industrial revolution, new techniques were adopted by forward-looking
men in the field of production, like Arkwright, Boulton, and Krupp.
In the American Civil War, the crucial steps toward war were taken
by members of the upper strata of society and not of the lower.

Second, the degree of rigidity will depend on the extent to which
there is a *latent fear of change* in the society in question. This fear
may stem from uncertainty as to the ultimate effects of change, so
that even peripheral and seemingly unimportant changes may sometimes be resisted because of the unpredictability of the final outcome.
Latent fear of change was an important influence in the attitudes of
the advocates of slavery in the South prior to the Civil War. Conversely, flexibility may be increased if dominant segments of society
have a well-established faith in the inevitability and beneficial effects
of change or, in other words, a faith in the inevitability of "progress."
It was this kind of doctrine that the social evolutionists of the late
nineteenth century preached with ardor.

Third, rigidity is increased if a society has little *surplus energy and
resources* for experimentation. If all human energy is devoted to
meeting immediate needs for subsistence, no matter what the reasons
for this condition may be, rigidities will be increased. Conversely, a
considerable surplus is conducive to the creation of opportunities for
alternative uses of time, energy, and resources. The relative lack of
surplus in the form of investment capital in the South prior to the
Civil War retarded industrial expansion and hence retarded the
development of types of enterprise incompatible with slavery. It contributed to prolongation of rigidities in the economy in general and
of slavery in particular. On the other hand, the surplus in the form
of savings for investment in England during the industrial revolution

meant that time could be taken from the manufacture of goods to meet current needs in order to turn out producers' goods, which in the long run would provide a greater supply of consumers' goods.

So important, indeed, is surplus and its effects on society that a striking convergence may be found between the peaks of civilization and peaks of economic well-being.[10] It seems clear that over long periods of time economic surplus makes possible techniques for extending man's control over nature, along with laws and institutions for regulating human relationships and the great artistic and intellectual achievements which in Western culture are the marks of civilization. Without surplus, members of a society have no time for contemplation, experimentation, or the exchange of ideas—the very wellsprings of change—and tend to remain in a static condition.

Fourth, rigidities in society depend in part on *physical environment* and in part on the *biological composition* of the population. Among other things, physical environment influences the extent to which surpluses may be created and the possibility of exchanging ideas with other persons and other societies. Desert societies, for example, seem to have changed much less than those in rich agricultural areas, particularly those in fertile valleys of navigable rivers. Similarly, biological factors may lead to rigidities if individuals are physically weak or inactive because of inherited body types, poor foods, or poor health, like the Pygmies or tsetse fly victims of Portuguese West Africa.

The preceding discussion does not lead to the conclusion that rigidities in culture and social structure present inviolable obstacles to change. On the contrary, such rigidities may contain elements that tend to undermine their own existence. There is much evidence, for example, that a rigidity such as a style in art tends to be fulfilled: artists employ it over a long period, develop it to a peak of considerable refinement, and ultimately revolt against it in their search for a new style that will more adequately meet their total demands, including the satisfaction they may acquire from self-expression.[11] In medieval scholasticism inquiry regarding orthodox religious beliefs contributed to a heterodoxy that ultimately weakened a rigidly organized Church. And in France of the *ancien régime* a rigidly established form of government created a body of criticism that contributed

[10] Shepard B. Clough, *The Rise and Fall of Civilization* (New York: McGraw-Hill Book Company, 1951).

[11] One of the best statements of this point is to be found in A. L. Kroeber, *Configurations of Culture Growth* (Berkeley: University of California Press, 1944).

to its undoing. Obviously rigidities have their antithetical aspects; in the illustrations given, the attacks on rigidities were creating a situation of flexibility.

Flexibility in a culture, as well as the range of opportunities, is of primary concern in analyzing general factors of change. But to these factors should be added a final consideration pertaining to the nature, scope, and rate of change. In any society, even a highly structured one, some ideologies or institutions are not considered to be very important and changes in them have little effect on elements deemed significant to the functioning and survival of that society. For example, styles in women's dress change with such rapidity in twentieth century American society that change itself has become institutionalized. Producers, distributors, and customers all expect change, plan for it, and adjust their behavior (inventories and purchasing patterns) to it without violent protest from anyone. Finally, fewer people offer resistance to changes that are gradual than to those that are sudden. Federal old age insurance in the United States, for example, was introduced with relatively little opposition because similar legislation had already come into existence in several of the states. Indeed, one may say that parts of a culture or social structure deemed unimportant change more readily than those deemed important, that the more closely an aspect of culture or social structure is tied in with other parts of society the greater the resistance to change will be, and that slow or evolutionary change is effected with less strain than sudden or revolutionary change.

BIOLOGICAL AND PHYSICAL FACTORS OF CHANGE

We have suggested that among the more important general factors of change in society are: (1) a wide range of alternative opportunities; (2) relative flexibility or looseness of structure in culture and social organization; and (3) lack of resistance because of the isolated character or gradualness of a change. We turn now to a consideration of more specific factors that operate directly to effect change—to what are frequently, though loosely, referred to as the "dynamic" factors in society. These dynamic factors or active agents of change are found in the four analytically isolable aspects of human activity; the biological, the physical, the social, and the cultural. In actuality, members of a society are subject to all these influences at the same time; nevertheless, the distinctions are useful in analysis.

The fact that the individual is an organism means that change can come from purely biological factors. Although the historian cannot study the gene patterns of individuals long dead, he should be aware that biologists hold that these patterns determine individual make-up and that changes in the patterns may affect the physical composition of a group. Furthermore, a certain amount of selective breeding takes place among humans as a result of biological, social, cultural, and physical environments, which may result in new body types. Similarly the human organism, like any other organism, requires food and oxygen, and the supply and use of these will affect its growth. Thus physical types may be altered by diet, even very dramatically, and such alterations may be a source of change. They may create hyperthyroid types who crave action and who are frequently the more dramatic leaders in society, or they may lead to a very weak group which does not bestir itself. But here a word of warning must be introduced. Changes in physical characteristics are difficult to ascertain and their effects on social and cultural behavior even more so. Also, the physical characteristics of persons within any large group vary enormously because of intermixture and differences in the diet and health of individuals. Hence it is quite erroneous uncritically to attribute to a group with certain common physical similarities, such as color of skin, similarities of a social and cultural character. This has been the fallacy of those who have propounded the doctrine of race.[12]

Change may also be effected by population movements, by changes in the total size of the population or in the relative size of component parts. Population aggregates are altered by the relation between births and deaths and by migration into and out of a society. The composition of a population may be changed, as has already been suggested, by the formation of new gene patterns or by diet and health experience, by a decline or extension of life expectancy, or by changes in the rate of growth. Such movements are certain to have an impact on social institutions and culture. For example, an increase in the population of the North prior to the Civil War was one of the factors encouraging capital formation and investment, so that the requirements of increased numbers could be met. In the South the increase in population probably operated to increase pressure on the more limited economic resources and contributed to tension among those competing for resources, particularly land suitable for raising cotton and tobacco. On the other hand, a decrease in population, or a

[12] For a more extended discussion see Gardner Murphy, *Personality: A Biosocial Approach to Origins and Structure.*

decline in the rate of population growth, may allow resources that
go into capital formation to be diverted in part to consumers' goods
—a trend that was visible in France prior to World War I. Changes
in the age composition of a population will alter the need for educational and other social services, competition of various kinds, the
burden of caring for increased numbers of unproductive children or
old people, and the proportion of the population capable of productive work or military service. Thus European migration of predominantly productive age groups into the North prior to the Civil
War contributed directly to the productivity and military strength
of that region.[13]

Another important agent of change is the physical environment,
although most changes in it are slow. In historic time there has apparently been little change in the climate of known portions of the earth.
But there is a good deal of archaeological evidence that at the end
of the last ice age, by one chronology some 20,000 years ago, the
steppes and tundras of Europe became temperate forests and the
prairies south of the Mediterranean and in Hither Asia were transformed into deserts with scattered oases and river valleys. In the latter
regions climatic changes led to the cultivation of grains and the
domestication of animals. This change had an enormous impact on
society, for settled agriculture requires radically different human relationships than those characteristic of food gathering.[14] In shorter
periods of time there have been few climatic changes of such magnitude, yet there may be successive years of drought or of abundant
rainfall. Even changes of the seasons from anticipated norms may
result in food shortages or oversupply which may affect population
aggregates, the composition of the population, migration, cultural and
societal relations, or important public policies.[15] For example, in
France poor crops in 1788 resulted in such shortages that in July 1789
the price of grain reached the highest point ever attained and contributed to the discontent of city workers. These urban elements lent
their support to a revolutionary movement which they had not
initiated.

[13] A. M. Carr-Saunders, *World Population: Past Growth and Present Trends*
(Oxford: Clarendon Press, 1936); Walter F. Willcox, *Studies in American Demog-
raphy* (Ithaca: Cornell University Press, 1940); and Joseph J. Spengler, *France Faces
Depopulation* (Durham: Duke University Press, 1938).

[14] Vere Gordon Childe, *What Happened in History* (New York: Penguin Books,
1942), Chapters 2–3.

[15] Ellsworth Huntington, *Mainsprings of Civilization*.

Other changes in physical environment, such as a shift in a river's course, the silting up of a harbor, or the destruction of a forest cover by fire from lightning, affect persons directly dependent on these natural conditions.

For the most part, however, at least in relatively modern times, changes in physical environment are the result of the actions of men rather than of nature and are hence primarily social and cultural. In this connection one should recognize that no product of nature can be considered a natural resource until man wants it for his use and has techniques for exploiting it. Thus, rich, swampy land is not a natural resource unless man can drain it and cultivate it; nor were coal, gold, or uranium ore of any importance until man wanted them and had means of using them. Such products of nature can be exhausted or altered by man. Some coal deposits and gold mines have been worked beyond any social usefulness, and a similar fate may in time befall the others.[16] Similarly, deforestation and overcropping can lead to lack of water, soil erosion, and barrenness, as they have in parts of the Near East and North Africa. Soil exhaustion from cotton cropping in parts of the South contributed to the drive of Southerners for more land to the west; and the concentration on agriculture in the South delayed the exploitation of coal and iron resources there and incidentally delayed the development of industry essential to the conduct of war.

Finally, attention should be called to the role of physical environment in change when a society moves to a new setting. In the past several waves of migration can be identified, such as the movement of the People of the Sea about 1200 B.C., the barbarian invasions of the Roman Empire, the emigration of Europeans overseas since 1500, and the westward movement in the United States. Through major migrations like these, peoples obtain access to entirely new natural resources, and the consequent changed relations of population to resources have societal effects. Trade provides access to new resources, also, and influences the behavior of people. Thus westward expansion in the United States prior to the Civil War not only accentuated sectional rivalry, but increased the economic potential of the North. And the development of trade between the South and Europe led the Southerners to an erroneous belief that cotton was king and could bring them needed products of industry, even in time of war.

16 Erich W. Zimmermann, *World Resources and Industries* (New York: Harper & Brothers, 1933), Part I.

CULTURAL AND SOCIAL FACTORS OF CHANGE

From this brief statement regarding biological and physical factors of change, it should be clear that social factors, which have to do with relationships of individuals and groups in society, and cultural factors, which have to do with the learnable and transmissible knowledge of society, become quickly involved in and condition the effects of any change. Even changes in the biological characteristics of a group will be affected by socially determined rules about mating and by transmissible knowledge that certain physical weaknesses, like hemophilia, may be inherited and should be avoided.

Social and cultural factors are responsible for most change in society and for most rapid change. Since they are made by man, they are more variable than biological and physical factors, and more readily subject to man's control. By means of them man can mitigate and within limits regulate the effects of natural forces. A biological tendency to increase the population may be offset by sociocultural considerations, for example, by a desire for small families. Even the effects of a prolonged drought may be minimized if there are abundant supplies of food elsewhere, means of transportation to the stricken area, and ways of inducing the holders of the supplies of food to part with them. In fact, one of the marks of civilization—of distance from animal savagery—is the control that man has established over nature.

Perhaps the most important concept for locating social and cultural factors of change is innovation. Innovations may be classified as they pertain to a society's (1) culture, (2) social institutions, (3) social groups, (4) foci of power, and (5) membership. No matter what the innovation is, it may be invented or developed within a society (autonomous origin) or it may be introduced from outside the society (external origin). But whatever the origin of an innovation, its adoption, adaptation, and diffusion will depend on the *total* environment in which it appears, that is, on whether or not and precisely how it fits into the total situation. The magnitude of its effect will be correlated with the extent to which it changes the more fundamental elements of a society. Rate of change can be measured by the speed with which the innovation is adopted and produces its effects. The direction of change will depend on the nature of the innovation and its effects.

Each of these aspects of an innovation needs further examination.

First let us consider the development of something new,[17] that is, the process of inventing and its products, inventions. Although these terms are ordinarily used to refer to the development of techniques, they are applicable to any sociocultural phenomena. An invention is usually the result of the gradual accretion of detailed knowledge of many kinds and from many sources, which makes possible a new and socially recognized way of thought or action. The process is usually slow at first, but gathers momentum as some definite stage of completion is envisaged. It may be impelled by some generally expressed need in society, or by the conscious efforts of individuals who believe that there is a need, or who gain satisfaction from the activity involved in inventing or innovating.

These points may be illustrated by almost any of the chief mechanical inventions of the eighteenth century. In the case of the steam engine, for example, progress was slow with the Savery engine and then with the Newcomen. By the time of Watt advance was more rapid, with many men working on the problem and nearly all drawing ideas from a diversity of sources. Finally, widespread adoption of the steam engine was impelled by new needs for cheap, mobile power. A similar account could be given of the cotton gin. The effects of both these inventions are well known. The steam engine has provided most of the mechanical power in our industrial society to date and in part has made that society possible. The cotton gin cheapened the cost of cotton, enabled it to compete more favorably with wool and linen, encouraged cotton planting in the South, and contributed to the extension and strengthening of the institution of slavery.

Invention, as has been implied, is seldom if ever the work of one man, although some historians and the patent laws tend to emphasize the opposite view. In fact, most great inventions—whether mechanical devices, ideas, or forms of social organization—have been arrived at almost simultaneously by independent workers.[18]

This would seem to indicate that invention is in part the result

[17] On this subject one can consult with profit: H. G. Barnett, *Innovation: The Basis of Cultural Change;* S. C. Gilfillan, *The Sociology of Invention;* William F. Ogburn, *Social Change* (New York: Viking Press, 1952); A. P. Usher, *A History of Mechanical Inventions* (New York: McGraw-Hill Book Company, 1929); Charles E. Merriam, *The Role of Politics in Social Change* (New York: New York University Press, 1936); Lewis Einstein, *Historical Change* (Cambridge: Cambridge University Press, 1946).

[18] Ogburn, *Social Change,* pp. 85–86.

of sociocultural factors. Yet we must not lose sight of the obvious: these factors work on and through individuals, and the particular endowments and training of individuals play a large role. It is not strange, for example, that intelligent and trained mathematicians like Newton and Leibnitz should have invented calculus almost simultaneously and independently, but it would have been strange if a hundred untrained peasants had invented it at the same time, or ever. Likewise, sociocultural forces largely explain the invention of the cotton gin. Many persons were working at the same time to produce a machine that could separate seeds from cotton, but all those persons were connected in one way or another with the cotton industry. Yet the inventors were not the untrained slave cotton pickers, but men like Eli Whitney who had considerable mechanical experience.

While the discovery of something new is called invention, the process by which such discoveries are utilized and culturally assimilated is known as innovation. Thus the discovery of nylon thread in the laboratory was an invention, but the production and sale of nylon fabrics represented innovation. Inventions become significant in processes of social change only when they reach the stage of innovation. One important factor in the process of innovation is the *range of opportunities for the communication of ideas.* If innovations come from the slow accretion of knowledge of many details, there must be extensive exchange of ideas regarding these details in order that their accumulation may take place. Similarly, in the case of borrowing from others, which is one major source of innovations, there must be extensive contacts among people of different cultures and societies before the advantages of something new impel its adoption. Innovations are consequently fostered in those cultures where knowledge may be stored by writing and where knowledge is easily transmitted by systems of communication. This fact helps to explain why innovations have come primarily from urban areas or thickly settled districts where a ready exchange of ideas and techniques has been possible and why borrowed innovations have usually been transmitted through commercial centers.[19] The introduction of slavery into the United States is a case in point. It was a borrowed institution, which came to be known by the English and Americans from their contacts with the Caribbean areas and South America. And slaves were first employed in the immediate vicinity of shipping centers.

[19] R. D. McKenzie, *The Metropolitan Community* (New York: McGraw-Hill Book Company, 1933); and Noel P. Gist and L. A. Halbert, *Urban Society* (New York: Thomas Y. Crowell Company, 1950).

ADOPTION AND DIFFUSION OF INNOVATIONS

Once the presence of an innovation is accounted for either by invention or borrowing, the social scientist is concerned with its adoption, adaptation, and diffusion. He asks whether the new way of thought or action is congenial to the society in question. Are its cultural and social structures flexible enough for acceptance of the innovation? Does it fit into the physical environment? Will its introduction be advantageous to leaders in positions of power? In brief, does the range of opportunities for making alternative decisions permit its being regarded with favor?

More specifically the social scientist may inquire whether the innovation is capable of eliciting a positive response from individuals and of rewarding them if they do respond positively. In general, an innovation that satisfies some primary drive, like hunger, thirst or sex, is more likely to be adopted than one that can satisfy only a minor, culturally created drive, such as to belong to a given social club. Thus, in a desert society a gadget for locating and obtaining water will have more chance of adoption than a portable phonograph. The abolition of slavery, itself an innovation, met opposition to some degree because of fear on the part of Southerners of violence from emancipated slaves.

Furthermore, an innovation that is in line with or similar to accepted social institutions, social organization, and culture patterns will have an easier path than one that is not compatible with them. It is well established that individuals perceive most readily and recall most easily those things that are most agreeable to them. The adoption by a society of a new way of thought or action will depend in part on the extent to which it relieves existing tensions in the society and hence is relatively agreeable to it.

In the expansion of Europe overseas, natives of India and China quickly accepted machine-made cotton textiles from Manchester, for there was little difference between machine-made and homemade cloth, but they did not quickly adopt European styles of dress or European ideas of religion. Also, in the industrialization of backward areas the textile industry was one of the first to become mechanized, in part because the procedures of manufacturing by machine were much like those used in handicraft production. The American Indian had a great fondness for trinkets, presumably because he felt pleasure from personal adornment; and he took easily to firearms because they were useful in his quest of game and his defense against enemies.

Another problem in the adoption and spread of an innovation relates primarily to methods of diffusion. One culture may be so powerful that it forces itself on others, as exemplified by much of Western European cultural imperialism during the last four centuries. Europe's economy, many of its techniques, its political ideas, and to some extent its religions have reached all corners of the earth. Through its prestige or physical force, it has impressed many of its features on others—and others have had to adjust to the situation as best they could. Contrariwise, the powerful culture or society is much more selective in its borrowings. Europe has taken such products as quinine, tobacco, the potato, cotton, and certain art styles from countries overseas, but it has borrowed comparatively little from their religions, forms of social organization, or methods of production. In transfers of either kind, however, and in the process of social acculturation to the importation, the innovation may be transformed into something far different from what it was in its place of origin. Thus Christianity has been completely transformed by some primitive tribes, and institutions of democratic government, like the electoral system, have at times degenerated into a physical contest of some kind.

In addition to the horizontal diffusion of innovations over a culture or several cultures, there is the problem of vertical diffusion. In every society there is some stratification of its members on the basis of wealth, profession, or power, and an innovation that satisfies one stratum may have little or no appeal to another. Many of the mechanical inventions of the industrial revolution were made by skilled workers, but the inventions themselves appealed more strongly to businessmen who might profit from their adoption than they did to workers. In this case diffusion was upward, but as the machines were put into use, they had effects on lower economic strata and profoundly altered their ways of living. Marxian socialism was of middle class origin and was diffused downward to those classes that it was presumably devised to benefit. Slavery appealed primarily to large plantation owners and was not extensively diffused downward in its economic aspects to the small farmer or small businessman.[20]

The diffusion of an innovation also has functional elements, that is, it affects first those who introduce or make it, then those who use it, and finally those who use its products. Farm tractors first affected inventors, entrepreneurs, and workers who made them. When they reached the farms, they replaced some alternate means of traction, probably horses or mules, and gradually reduced the need for teamsters, harness makers, and blacksmiths. Then, as the use of tractors decreased costs

[20] On these questions see Sorokin, *Social and Cultural Dynamics, op. cit.*

of producing grain, the price of grain was reduced, the consumption of grain by humans and animals increased, and the well-being of consumers improved. The introduction of slavery first affected masters and slaves personally, then the supply of products grown, particularly cotton and tobacco, then the consumers of the products, and finally the part of American society that took sides on the slavery issue. These effects may be classified as primary, secondary, tertiary, etc.

Sometimes a society develops a group of persons who specialize in so increasing their range for making alternative decisions that they become specialists in taking advantage of innovations. In business, such persons are often referred to as entrepreneurs. During the industrial revolution those who undertook to put inventions to practical use were merchants or producers who had capital and an attitude that permitted taking a risk in hope of gain. The innovators of slavery were traders and shippers, in the first instance, and in the second, landowners who had enough means or enough need to encourage speculation on a new form of labor.[21]

RATE, SIZE, AND DIRECTION OF CHANGE

Change, no matter what its origin, will vary in rate, size, and direction according to the character of the innovation, to the nature of the total environment (social, cultural, biological, and physical) in which it occurs, and to the leadership that is given it. Slavery in the South, as has been noted, was given constructive leadership by persons in positions of power and came into a generally congenial environment. The direction that it took was influenced primarily by social, cultural, and economic considerations, and these forces modified it profoundly in certain areas. The rate at which it was adopted was determined by similar forces, which came into sharp relief in the struggle over new slave territory.

With respect to the rate of change, social science has developed hypotheses concerning lag. The concept of lag comes from the contention that in Western culture most sociocultural changes have been caused by prior innovations in techniques. As changes in economic structure caused by techniques occur, they have their impact on other

[21] For the role of the innovating specialist in the field of economics, see B. S. Keirstead, *The Theory of Economic Change* (Toronto: Macmillan Company, 1948); Joseph A. Schumpeter, "Theoretical Problems of Economic Growth," *Journal of Economic History*, 7(suppl.):1–9 (1947); and Colin Clark, *The Conditions of Economic Progress* (London: Macmillan and Co., 1951).

aspects of society and culture, which may eventually adjust to them. There is a lag between the invention and the adjustment. Thus the invention of cotton textile machinery gave an impetus to cotton growing; cotton cultivation required more labor; slaves were used for this labor; and certain prevailing theories regarding the equality of man or the golden rule lagged behind or never did become adjusted to the institution of slavery, especially in the North.

Hypotheses of cultural lag are stimulating, but the concept is too narrow to have general applicability. Even in the case of an invention, it tends to minimize the sociocultural forces demanding the technique, the accumulation of capital necessary to launch the technique, or the vigorous entrepreneurial leadership that precedes the finding of a new means of performing a given task. In fact, many examples could be found where techniques seem to lag behind sociocultural demand.[22] Furthermore, the concept of lag is logically questionable, for if changes are taking place simultaneously in two institutions in diametrically opposite directions, it can hardly be said that one is lagging behind the other. Yet in spite of such criticisms the concept has been useful; it has called attention to the tensions that arise from change and to adjustments necessary to relieve them. This has led, for example, to a consideration of "peaceful change"—of how adjustments to change in one part of the sociocultural environment can be brought into harmony with others so that tensions will not increase to the point where they are dealt with violently.

In this connection attention should be called to the development in social science fields of techniques for measuring and analyzing social attitudes and tensions. From responses obtained in interviews with carefully selected samples of members of various groups estimates are made of the typical attitudes held by the members of the groups on specific issues, the functions served by these attitudes, how they are rationalized, and how firmly they are held. Although use of these techniques is in its infancy and cannot yet be of much service to historians, it has already made considerable contributions to our knowledge. It can identify and measure attitudes now held, even though it cannot predict with accuracy what attitudes people may hold in the future. It has confirmed an earlier belief in the strong influence of face-to-face groups on the opinions held by their members. It has shown how events rather than propaganda influence people. It has supported the concept of facility of change in societies with flexible

22 See Ogburn, *Social Change*, pp. 269–270.

sociocultural structures. And through correlation of respondents' attitudes with their economic status, their cultural background, and their
social and power positions, it suggests why certain people think as
they do. In brief, these techniques are research tools which can greatly
facilitate and improve studies of change.[23] The data provided may
be of great importance to future historians.

The magnitude and direction of change, as has already been suggested, depend on the nature of the change and the total environment
in which it takes place. In analyzing the size and direction of change,
the social scientist is confronted with tracing effects through primary,
secondary, tertiary, and succeeding stages and with a complexity of
forces of which the original innovation is only one. Here, more specialized social science knowledge is needed, as well as extensive data
and good judgment. What was the size of the institution of slavery;
what was the magnitude of its effects on the South and on Southern
policy toward the North; in what direction was it moving, toward
liquidation or intrenchment; and what relation did it have to the
actual outbreak of war? It is precisely with such complex problems as
these that historians struggle. Incidentally, they are the ones that lead
to differences of judgment among historians. Only through detailed
analysis along lines already suggested does it seem possible to arrive
at more general scientific knowledge of human behavior in the past.

By employing social science concepts and methods the historian
should be able more adequately to describe changes in the past, to
analyze the forces that caused them, and to measure their more important effects. From his study of change he can suggest within broad
tolerances some of the primary and secondary effects of a proposed
"innovation" in a given setting—and he can indicate reasoned possibilities and probabilities that may be useful in the formation of public
and private policies. If control over physical and sociocultural environment constitutes the distance that separates civilized humans from
the savage, then the historian through his knowledge of human affairs
in the past can do much to indicate the conditions necessary to the
attainment of higher levels of civilization in the future.

[23] See, for example, Paul F. Lazarsfeld, Bernard Berelson, and Hazel Gaudet, *The
People's Choice* (2nd ed.; New York: Columbia University Press, 1948).

6 METHODS: THEORY AND PRACTICE

That practice comes before theory is one of the oldest of rules. But research in history and other social sciences has reached the point at which it is important to distinguish between older practices, still highly useful, and newer practices offering the prospect of expanding knowledge. The first sections of this chapter present various suggestions for a historian's theory of historical knowledge.

DOCUMENTARY METHOD

Historians work so much with documents and entertain such respect for documentary method that they sometimes consider it the only historical method. Those who accept this view are likely to start their research—contrary to general procedure in social science—not with a problem, but with a body of documents, such as a newly published collection or series, or private papers newly opened. A doctoral candidate may start work on such documents with no particular concepts in mind, and no hypotheses. He intends simply to "find out what is in the documents."

Such a procedure may be a consequence of the Ranke tradition of extreme empiricism: attention to "facts" which are supposed to speak for themselves. Alternatively it may signify not hostility to theory but reliance on induction alone, on the supposition that one looks first at facts and then "discovers" the theory or generalization. The early "scientific" schools coupled such views with disrespect for deductive reasoning from general premises. Whatever the philosophic rationale for such an attitude, the consequences for method are the same; one does not start with a problem, nor with any well-considered principles of selection.

Social science concepts and methods suggest a change in the order of procedure. Without any disrespect for "what the facts show," the historian who uses these concepts and methods draws no clear line between induction and deduction. He prefers neither one nor the other, nor is he concerned whether induction precedes or follows deduction.[1]

---

[1] See John Stuart Mill's denial that induction must precede deduction in Morton G. White, "The Attack on the Historical Method," *Journal of Philosophy*, 42:325 (June 7, 1945).

He does not ordinarily start with a collection of documents, but with a historical situation that presents a problem. He then formulates hypotheses posing questions about this problem. At this stage, but not before, he begins to search for documentary evidence that suggests answers to the questions raised.

Social science procedure is already relatively common in historical investigation. Historical definition of the nature of a document has gradually been altered. For example, the range of meaning has been enlarged to include such data as statistical series. Thus, in seeking the "facts," the historian is not necessarily looking for self-evident facts that appear in the traditional "documents" of history. He may be looking for correlations that can be detected and measured only by special techniques of analysis. The concepts and methods of social science increase the range of verification by documentation and permit the historian to go beyond raw data and direct "testimony." Increasingly, since the era of Ranke, social science has had marked influence on historians in stimulating scientific analysis of the traditional documents. Historical method has made great strides in determining the authenticity and original meaning of written records. The two primary approaches, analysis of internal evidence and investigation of external evidence—comparison with other documents and study of the social context surrounding the document—are achievements that lie in the realm of the scientific.[2] Well tested and long familiar, they are empirical modes of appeal to facts and are basic for cumulative analysis.

When dealing with multiple factors in a broad area or over a long period, the historian almost always resorts to summary generalizations. For these he may rely on monographs and research by many other historians; but he depends also on what is variously called "insight," "historical imagination," and "a sense of history." Such generalized impressions regarding historical tendency and cause and effect are usually in the category of an expert guess. Behind them may be a long process of study, knowledge of many documents, and a slow maturing of thought. Experts in all branches of knowledge are forced to make such guesses. Social science method suggests simply that such insights represent only the first stage in the process of formulating a hypothesis; and that the resulting tentative hypothesis should be tested.

No historian can test all flashes of insight. Lack of time and the

[2] For guides to procedure see Louis Gottschalk, *Understanding History*, Chapters 6, 7.

variability and complexity of historical materials often force the historian to pose interpretations without testing them. To that extent the historian remains in the tradition of the humanities. His insight is that of the expert in history; but it is an impressionistic generalization, nevertheless, and in terms of methodology is like the affirmations of those who are content to state an idea either because it inspires belief or because it seems a reasonable inference.

The ideal of objectivity presupposes that major hypotheses should be tested. Yet it would retard the advance of knowledge were it insisted that no hypothesis should be presented before it had been fully tested and documented. Great theories in the physical sciences are not only presented before verification but in themselves can never be completely verified. Such theories, however, make it possible to predict and to draw inferences that can be tested. Hypotheses should be presented if they suggest explanations; and if they do indeed yield fruitful suggestions, there will be those who will test them. Nevertheless, a distinction should be made between an unsupported hypothesis and a tentative hypothesis for which a considerable body of data is presented. We may classify a very tentative hypothesis by saying that "it goes beyond the data"; but we should bear in mind that any large hypothesis must go beyond immediately available data and is never completely verifiable.

The documentary method of historians is reflected in the quoting or citing of statements to illustrate the pros and cons of moot points. In presenting a particular thesis, such as Turner's theory of the influence of the frontier on American history,[3] citations are selected in terms of their relevance to the thesis. While recognizing the value of monographs devoted to a special thesis, the historical craft has been conscious of the methodological inadequacy of single explanations. Nevertheless, it is not yet the usual practice of historians explicitly to pose *alternative* hypotheses and compare and test them in the light of correlations found in the data. Presumably, before the final report is written, various alternative hypotheses have actually been rejected. But a historian infrequently records what he regards as negative findings.

This discussion implies that the traditional documentary method does not automatically give protection against untested assumptions

[3] Frederick J. Turner, "The Significance of the Frontier in American History," *Annual Report of the American Historical Association, 1893*, pp. 199–227; *The Frontier in American History* (New York: Henry Holt and Company, 1921).

nor guarantee substantial hypotheses. Facts do not "speak for themselves." Concepts do not "emerge" from the evidence. Common sense
interpretations are the first, not the last, step in analysis. The use of
general social science concepts by historians encourages a cumulative
refinement of analysis by means of continuous explicit testing of interpretations. Social science theories rest on a formidable body of
analysis and investigation and, when applied to historical data, may
well be more valid than an impression or assumption based merely
on "a sense of history."

SYSTEMATIC PROCEDURE

When history takes its place in social science, research tactics are
developed in accordance with a systematic procedure. As has been
stated, the first stage in research typically begins with recognition of
a problem, that is, the investigator concludes that previous explanations of a phenomenon are unsatisfactory or that more remains to be
said. Thus, recognition of a problem starts *from knowledge,* not from
a random decision to study something. It may be the initial stage of an
inductive inference from previous knowledge; or it may be a deductive
inference from theory. Not all problems are equally important, and
the various branches of social science may well aid the investigator in
deciding which problems are fundamental, which are interesting but of
marginal importance, which are fictitious, and which are metaphysical
and insoluble by historical data.

Definition of the problem and formulation of questions or hypotheses are crucial because these determine the direction of the investigation. Defining the problem means conceptualizing it and delimiting it
in a preliminary way; posing questions or hypotheses carries this process
further. Having defined the problem, a tentative frame of reference or
conceptual scheme *relevant* for the problem (i.e., one that directs
attention to appropriate types of data) is set up for exploratory purposes. From this conceptual scheme the questions or working hypotheses that can be tried out as possible solutions of the problem are
derived. These may be simple questions not yet in the form of tentative
generalizations; or they may be general theoretical propositions formulated as hypothetical explanations of the problem. The latter may
already have considerable reliability if they have empirical support in
other contexts or situations. They may be drawn from a thesis developed in previous study, or they may be deductions from reliable
theory developed elsewhere in history or in any of the social sciences.

In short, to study history in terms of *problems, some* theoretical framework and *some* working hypotheses are unavoidable. But theoretical schemes and working hypotheses, even if not selected on the basis of certain knowledge, need not be selected at random.

The next step, elaborating hypotheses, is simply a search for unifying principles or ways of collecting, organizing, and asking questions of data. Hypotheses must be elaborated to develop their implications and put them in testable form. Elaboration consists of combining hypotheses with other known factors relevant to the particular historical situation that we are studying. We develop implications by conceiving logical consequences of our hypotheses: how they should actually work out in history. Methodological confusion will result if hypotheses are not sharpened and stated in a form that can be tested by data; and logical fallacies will result if they are not stated carefully, so as to be self-consistent. Definitions must be constant and identify the same thing as the same thing. Multiple working hypotheses, however, may be illogical, i.e., self-contradictory. Logically, true hypothetical affirmations must be consistent with other true statements. When all our working hypotheses are not consistent with each other, we know that we have *alternative contradictory hypotheses.* This is welcome on the principle that the more plausible explanations we consider, the greater the likelihood that we will find the stronger one. Analysis of data should eliminate the weaker explanations. One other principle of logic applies: appropriateness or relevance. Are the hypothetical explanations central or even germane to the study? Do they stick to the delimitation, or does the delimitation itself verge on triviality? Could the delimitation produce something less trivial?

In actual practice, sharpening of hypotheses to make them testable is not immediate. Research is not mechanical. As Dewey long ago pointed out, hypotheses are not first fully developed, then tested and accepted or rejected.[4] The initial delimitation and first crude formulations of hypotheses supply a principle of selection by which to begin collection and organization of data. Full development of each hypothesis is a result of a series of testings and modifications. Thus in its full development a hypothesis has evolved in the light of specific data.

Analysis of data involves the process of *verification* or "testing by observation." Once the evidence is collected, it is so arranged and so classified that one can apply various tests of working hypotheses.

[4] John Dewey and others, *Studies in Logical Theory* (Chicago: University of Chicago Press, 1903), p. 182.

Beard's hypothesis that economic interests affected political decisions, for example, led him to classify economic interests of the framers of the Constitution. Then he asked questions of the data as to correlations between specific interests and specific political decisions. While Beard's actual conclusions may have assumed additional presuppositions and hypotheses not explicitly stated, his method at least is sound in principle. Analysis of the evidence shows that we must reject or accept our hypothesis, or that we must modify and sharpen our questions. We thus analyze the *extent of verification*. We have predicted certain consequences or causal relations. Do our classifications of facts and correlations between data substantiate our hypothetical affirmations as to the structure of the situation, relations between occurrences, or tendencies in a movement? Verification, of course, is not final proof. It merely tends to confirm the hypothesis. Other hypotheses may appear, and conflicts between them may eventually be resolved by more inclusive and powerful hypotheses that explain apparent inconsistencies.[5]

Sometimes there is confusion as to whether economic "laws," such as those of the classical school concerning supply and demand or the wage fund, are directly concerned with empirical verification. They are not. They contain no empirical content and are regarded as "pure theory." An example, given by T. W. Hutchison,[6] is the assumption that "under perfect competition firms are of optimum size." Such a statement represents an attempt to insure that definitions of concepts are consistent with each other, and to make clear the relationships between the definitions. The process involves tautological deductive logic, a kind of circular reasoning in which the conclusions are assumed from the beginning in the original assumptions made in the definitions. Such definitions yield "inevitable" laws but, because of the lack of empirical content, tell nothing about new facts. *Definitions are arbitrary, a matter of convenience and consistency; no question of their empirical truth or falsity arises.* But definitions may be questioned. Are they precise or vague, useful or useless, self-consistent or self-contradictory?

In actual economic research, *empirical* generalizations are employed,

[5] See Abraham Edel, *The Theory and Practice of Philosophy* (New York: Harcourt, Brace and Company, 1946), pp. 69–74, especially the section on "extent of verification."

[6] T. W. Hutchison, *The Significance and Basic Postulates of Economic Theory*, Chapter 2.

and their truth or falsity is tested by the usual process of an appeal to evidence. Gresham's law, the principle of diminishing returns, and the theory of the relationship of consumption to income (consumption function) are not "pure theory"; they are examples of inductive empirical generalizations. As such, they are subject to verification.

Historians may observe from the experience in economics that controversy over definitions does not necessarily involve research questions turning upon empirical verification; and that definitions based on assumptions suggest new concepts of relationships but, since they lack empirical content, are not in themselves "reality" and yield no new knowledge. Definitions and propositions stating how definitions are interrelated are not empirically verifiable; they describe merely the rules according to which certain words are to be used. Empirical generalizations, on the other hand, are verifiable by reference to the evidence, according to the principles of scientific demonstration.

SCIENTIFIC VERIFICATION

If historians develop further the critical standards and methodological skills necessary for cumulative analysis, they will acquire corresponding intellectual habits. Simple proof by the documentary method of quoting testimony may not serve when dealing with larger questions of theory. Because the analytical methods and the logic of scientific "proof" do not always receive attention in history courses, a brief summary may suggest the value of experimenting with ways of verifying that supplement documentary procedure.[7] Logicians have defined various categories of verification. According to one, these are considered among the most important:

1. *Observation and Experimentation.*—This involves making a detailed study of the data on hand, gathering more data, or performing an experiment of some kind, all with the definite purpose of finding out whether the deduction which is being tested really holds. . . .

[7] The dearth of critiques by historians is apparent in the citations given. Some recent works in philosophy make reference to history, and many recent articles by historians reveal an interest in such critiques and a disposition to re-examine fundamentals. See other references in this chapter, and the following: P. W. Bridgman, *The Logic of Modern Physics* (New York: Macmillan Company, 1946) ; Charles K. Ogden and I. A. Richards, *The Meaning of Meaning* (New York: Harcourt, Brace and Company, 1946); James MacKaye, *The Logic of Language* (Hanover: Dartmouth College Publications, 1939); Carroll C. Pratt, *The Logic of Modern Psychology* (New York: Macmillan Company, 1939).

2. *Mathematical Calculation.*—When quantitative matters are involved mathematical calculations may be made and the facts shown to be either consistent or inconsistent with these computations. This way of verifying is frequently combined with experiment or observation, the calculations being regarded as a more exact and detailed interpretation of the deduction. Sometimes such mathematical elaborations of a deduction furnish the basis of a *prediction* of the precise way in which something will happen in nature. When such a theoretical prediction is later verified, the proof of the hypothesis from which it has been deduced is highly conclusive.

3. *Statistical Verification.*—Closely allied to mathematical calculation is statistical enumeration. When experiment is out of the question a statistical study may be made for the purpose of ascertaining whether the deduction always or generally holds. This may also bring into play the method of sampling.

4. *Verification by Elimination.*—An hypothesis may be strengthened by eliminating all competing hypotheses. The negative verification of competing hypotheses becomes a positive verification of the hypothesis which cannot be eliminated. To be sure other evidence can usually be found favoring such hypotheses, but elimination greatly strengthens the remaining hypothesis. Here again, . . . negation is shown to be highly significant in the growth of knowledge.

5. *Verification by Disjunctive Reasoning.*—Sometimes the hypothesis is verified by showing that it is the only one consistent with what is already known in the field of knowledge to which the data under investigation belong. The reasoning may take the form of a disjunctive syllogism—either this hypothesis is true or else what we know in this field is false. But what we know in this field is not false and hence this hypothesis is true. Consistency with previous knowledge in its field is always an excellent criterion of the truth of any hypothesis. That is why scientists always try to show that the hypothesis which they defend fits in with what we know better than any of the competing hypotheses.

In actual research scientists combine, in one way or another, all of these methods of verifying hypotheses. Hence it is a mistake to think of them as being mutually exclusive. The scientist verifies his deductions in any way .hat he can.[8]

Methods and Logic of Science

Science has developed by *cumulative analysis*. As a result of this process the investigator can accept the principles and correlations more

[8] Daniel S. Robinson, *Illustrations of the Methods of Reasoning* (New York: D. Appleton and Company, 1927), pp. 186–188; quoted by permission of Appleton-Century-Crofts.

adequately verified by his predecessors, and go on to a more advanced stage of analysis. Whether historical scholarship can demonstrate a significant degree of cumulative analysis is a fundamental question. The growth of cumulative analysis in the natural sciences has been much swifter than in the social sciences; and the scope of this development in the latter has been much more limited. Yet there is evidence that various processes in human affairs can be and have been subjected to very considerable analysis of a cumulative kind. Committee discussions with outside experts confirmed the impression that the most portentous development in modern social science is pioneering work in providing a more coherent basis for cumulative theory. One of the conditions for the development of cumulative analysis is an understanding of its logic and its methods.

Six aspects of the logic and methods of science are particularly relevant for discussion of cumulative analysis in social science.

1. *Fundamental for scientific discovery are respect for and use of theory.* Theorizing, by parallel use of large speculations (theories) and particular conjectures (tentative hypotheses), is the necessary and characteristic procedure in making scientific explanations. By the use of theory the scientist enlarges his intellectual universe. By introducing new hypotheses, he makes possible the investigation of causal relations involving new factors and new data. The method permits cumulative study of factual patterns previously not recognized. Larger inductive theories are a kind of conjectural synthesis. They are achieved by insight based on previous observation of apparent inconsistencies between existing theories and specific facts. They are subsequently made into a reasoned theory by inductive inference as to the characteristic order or system by which the phenomena are related. Inductive theory is reasoned speculation, moving from partial knowledge of some particulars to abstract theory of the whole to which the particulars appear to belong. It amounts to an inference that what has been observed in certain concrete occurrences may be affirmed as characteristic of a whole system of interrelated phenomena. The idea of the given system thus becomes a concept, an analytical device for classifying and studying relations between certain phenomena.

2. *Testable hypotheses and factual support for them are essential for warrantable conclusions.* Testable hypotheses are precise and limited, and predict specific relationships or occurrences under particular conditions. Methodological errors can be reduced by defining

procedures in operational terms, developing hypotheses that can be tested, and recognizing concepts as abstractions.[9]

3. *Since general theories are not testable directly or as a whole, they are confirmed piecemeal, indirectly, by the use of deductive hypotheses.* In deductive method, one begins with general abstract theory, predicts or deduces some of its particular consequences, then tests them against relevant particular data. It is not the deduction alone that is tested but the consistency and reliability of the original general theory. As techniques of deductive proof are refined, scientists discover more and more exceptions and have to qualify general laws arrived at by inductive inference.

4. *Most scientific hypotheses and theories are "working hypotheses," or estimates of probabilities, not definitive statements of certainties.* That a working hypothesis is provisional does not indicate that it is unscientific. On the contrary, science could not proceed at all without theoretical propositions of this tentative character. In science a hypothesis is sometimes assumed even when the investigator does not believe in it, in order to trace consequences of the hypothesis and *disprove* its accord with facts known or discoverable. A negative correlation has as much value in advancing knowledge as a positive correlation. A verified hypothesis may achieve status as an empirical law, but many hypotheses are not capable of complete verification. Even so, they continue to be employed tentatively as working hypotheses, unless an alternative hypothesis is accepted provisionally as a more consistent explanation of a wider range of facts and a more fruitful guide to further investigation.

5. *Theories are used or discarded, depending on the consequences derived from them.* This is the revisionary self-corrective process basic to cumulative analysis.

6. *Theory that runs beyond the established data is the source of fertility in cumulative scientific analysis.* Pure induction to discover causal relations by the rules of classical logic (Baconian induction) can show correlations of known facts and will always suggest a limited hypothesis as an explanation of these known facts. But one must go beyond the hypothesis based strictly on empirical knowledge; one must postulate a larger theory, partly a priori, reaching beyond known facts.

[9] See Bridgman, *op. cit.;* also Hans Vaihinger, *The Philosophy of 'As If'* (trans. C. K. Ogden; New York: Harcourt, Brace and Company, 1924) on the danger of confusing fictional concepts with testable hypotheses that affirm realities.

It is the larger theory rather than the limited hypothesis that is fertile in predicting new phenomena, previously unobserved, and in producing new concepts. Baconian induction, by itself, has not proved very fertile in physical science. For example, the fundamental laws of chemistry were empirical laws based on regularities or known ratios that occurred in combinations of elements. When theorists went beyond, postulating certain properties in given atomic structures, chemists deduced or predicted new types of behavior and interaction and tested their theoretical predictions by experimental study of the data relevant to the newer formulation.

These considerations are of primary importance if historians are to stimulate the advancement of cumulative research.

CUMULATIVE ANALYSIS

To give impetus to the process of cumulative analysis is, in the opinion of the Committee, one of the most important ends to be achieved by the use of social science methods in history. To the extent that historical research successfully embodies scientific method, the results will be cumulative. Since the sixteenth century the people of Western culture have assumed that man accumulates knowledge. Specialists on scientific method, however, have long insisted on a distinction between the halting growth of knowledge by accretion and the more continuous growth of knowledge by cumulative analysis. Many classical historical writings, together with literary and philosophical masterpieces, were superb examples of art of surpassing importance. But wherever lack of theoretical standards prevented determination of empirical reliability, there could be only a discontinuous and fragmentary accretion of knowledge. Discoveries were in fact forgotten. Sometimes they reappeared or were rediscovered independently. Writers in fields dominated by contemplative approaches might be "influenced" by predecessors, but each author started afresh, relying less on previous theories and concepts than on a vague climate of opinion and a personal point of view.

Requirements for cumulative research have already been indicated. Findings on a given problem must be sufficiently tenable to be worthy of acceptance as a working basis for further research. Not all interpretations and theories that "win acceptance," however, are worthy of it. Cumulative error, gossip, rumor, and scandal at times win acceptance. The requirement for scientific and cumulative research is that the criteria for general acceptance are not arbitrary. If X conducts a scientific experiment and reaches certain conclusions, which Y questions, then Y has only to repeat the experiment to see if he reaches the same conclusions. In social science, similarly, the criterion for acceptance is not the prestige of the preceding investigator; the test is whether another investigator, confronted with the same evidence and observing the same rules of logic, will obtain the same results. This principle is not vitiated by the fact that a social scientist, analyzing not only the same evidence but a larger range of evidence involving more cases, may come to a more general explanation that modifies the conclusions of the preceding investigations. Such cross-checking of results is an exemplification of cumulative analysis and its essential revisionary, self-corrective character. The critical standards that historians have developed provide the means to determine when they can accept previous findings and thus "build on and advance their predecessors' work." It is on the basis of such critical standards that Hutchison speaks of "steady secular piecemeal agreement" and a "cumulative, international, impersonal, and 'coral-reef-like' growth" of knowledge.[10]

Tenable theory has developed cumulatively in historical study of many problems. The cumulative effect appears when historians turn from the unique and individual to analyze structures and processes. There are really many working theories in historical explanations of regularized relationships and continuing processes. Turner's frontier hypothesis inspired a large body of valuable work. The concept of the industrial revolution similarly led to a cluster of working hypotheses; general assumptions as to the nature of the industrial revolution and its impact on history are now frequently made.

Historians have already adopted techniques conducive to cumulative discovery. They do not ordinarily conceive themselves as starting *de novo* with respect to concepts and theory. To explore the literature on the problem chosen for investigation and consider the theories of previous investigators is normal procedure. Historians, to be sure, object to "too much presupposition"; some appear fearful of being "theoretical." There is inevitably bad theory as well as good, and much that passes for historical theorizing is naive, unsystematic, and arbitrary. Objection to that is well founded. But those who object to theory as such must accept the onus of showing how historical propositions can attain the status of demonstrable truth without it. Theory is not necessarily bad because it is hypothetical, tentative, and not yet conclusively demonstrated or rejected.

[10] Hutchison, *op. cit.,* p. 7.

Hesitation to engage in "theoretical" treatment may be in part an effect of graduate training. The logic and methods of science have not generally been considered relevant for historical research. Notions of inductive and deductive method often remain fuzzy in students' minds. Yet, while the idea of the induction of "laws" has little appeal in the historical profession, there is a common sense belief in the validity of historical principles of limited scope. If the idea of inducing laws or complete theory has seemed too ambitious, the idea of evolving a theoretical synthesis has not. A semantic difficulty may exist here. Historians invariably develop conjectural explanations and interpretative syntheses, involving concepts as to the general characteristics of a movement, structure, or process in history. Such provisional syntheses constitute theory, even complex theory, derived inductively from knowledge of some of the parts and designed to make up for the lack of acceptable general knowledge of the whole. The provisional theoretical synthesis must still be checked by making particular deductions and applying them in the form of testable hypotheses. Synthesis is theory, and it is elaborated by historians both inductively and deductively.

Cumulative research is not appropriate for all types of intellectual activity. The great works of medieval scholastics and modern theologians certainly exhibit continuous elaboration and modification, and this process might perhaps be called cumulative. But the "truth of reason" has long been distinguished from empirical truth. The basis for cumulative analysis of this type is the unraveling of a logical system. This is not what is meant by cumulative research. One would hardly apply the latter term, for example, to the complex windings of Marxian dogma. It is of first importance in Marxian dialectics that each new proposition asserted to be true must be logically consistent with the words of the master; it is a secondary consideration whether or not the words have any empirical validity. Similarly the drawing of inferences from philosophical theories of history, designed to yield the "inevitable laws" of historical change, is not cumulative research, despite the tightest logic making it internally consistent. Great transcendental conceptions of the historical process, such as Hegel's, imposed on history from outside the realm of empirical knowledge, have never successfully been brought inside that realm. Cumulative research is possible only when each successive step forward can be tested by observation and experience. We must distinguish sharply between those propositions that can and those that cannot be proved false, that is, between those that can and that cannot be tested empirically.

Further, cumulative analysis does not and should not characterize all fields of interest to historians. It is not necessary for the development of cumulative analysis that all investigators be interested solely in the scientific. Nor must all historians think alike or feel obliged to treat history as a social science. For many it is not congenial to work with methods and theories of social science. Their disposition may be to regard history as a form of knowledge about the concrete, unique, and individual. Or they may cherish history as a literary and aesthetic form, recreating pictorially the life, romance, color, or tragedy of the past. Or they may be concerned with moral judgments of historical tendency. These are human interests and serve important social purposes.

Should cumulative analysis come to distinguish historical research, it will not be as the result of the findings of any committee. With respect to important specific problems, it might be advanced by group research adequately financed. But otherwise, as cumulative analysis develops in the historical field, it must proceed from the will, energy, and intellects of historians as a professional group. The immediate responsibility, if it is to be taken as such, is for historians, equipped by temperament and training, to demonstrate cumulative potentials. The ultimate responsibility lies with the community of scholars in all the social sciences. Cumulative discovery requires the work of many, who build on the work of their predecessors and in turn furnish a body of analysis from which their successors proceed cumulatively to a more advanced stage of substantive knowledge and procedure.

OBJECTIVITY, CERTAINTY, AND VALUES

Analysis of values and of other philosophical ideas as they appear in historical data presents no special problem. Value judgments made by historians, on the other hand, raise questions as to objectivity and certainty, and the functions of historical inquiry.

The debate over subjective factors in historical interpretation may now be outdated but it has caused confusion. The modern rediscovery of cultural relativism has led some to urge the elimination of values; it has led others to view history as an "act of faith." The one school assumed that values involved uncertainty, and that certainty could be attained only by objectivity. The other refused to deny historians a modest role among the guardians of cultural values, but at the same time despaired of achieving the certainty ascribed to physical science. The constructive contribution of the debate was to stress the importance of critical self-knowledge and to dispose of the supposition that a bare account of particular events was "history as it actually happened." No one now supposes that past history in its totality is recoverable, and few believe that "facts speak for themselves."

Contrary to the assertion frequently made by those outside the scientific disciplines, a set of interrelated hypotheses is the best check against unconscious bias. Psychologists have demonstrated in many ways the necessity of reference points for the avoidance of affect. In one such demonstration a person is asked to look through a peephole into a black box in which there is suspended a pinpoint of light, too weak to illuminate its surroundings. When asked in which direction the light is moving, the observer will almost invariably indicate a direction, although actually the light is motionless and the perception of motion comes wholly from suggestion. But if a thin line of light is admitted at the bottom of the box, a reference base, no one can be deluded into seeing movement. In the same way a preliminary set of categories and hypothetical relationships acts as a check against which the character of new data can be seen. If the data fail to fit, or move in an unexpected direction, this is at once apparent. Without such an explicit scheme the data are likely to be subconsciously selected, or catalogued on the basis of implicit or surreptitious assumptions not subject to a conscious process of analysis and rectification.

Objectivity need not be equated with certainty and completeness of knowledge. Science does not depend on full certainty, nor do scientists confuse objectivity with completeness of knowledge. The scientist, moreover, may be quite objective and as impassioned as he pleases in hoping to find evidence to prove or disprove some particular theory.[11] Objectivity requires us to be prepared on the basis of the evidence to abandon our most cherished hypotheses. One must, therefore, distinguish the subjective element in objective investigation to prevent distortion through bias. Distortion does not necessarily follow even though values influence the choice of hypotheses and the selection of data.

A *concept of importance,* as Whitehead calls it, is central to principles of selection. The problem selected, the hypotheses to be tested, the data, and the generalization are all conditioned by a concept of importance. Such a concept relates to subjective motives and ideas of the desirable, but this is not a commitment to values as against evidence. The generalizations evolved must still submit to tests of relevance and of consistency with the evidence. There are also rules of

11 C. H. Waddington, *The Scientific Attitude* (rev. ed.; West Drayton, England: Penguin Books, 1948), pp. 30, 32–35.

logic such as identity and noncontradiction. And there is the additional and difficult requirement that the selection of facts should be representative, a problem of theory and practice to which historians need to give greater attention.[12] These are all modes of objectivity. In logical terms a selection can be made from a list of factual statements known to be true without doing violence to the evidence. If the factual statements are true, selection is warrantable: "Any part of a true conjunction remains true." Thus, two different selections from the same body of facts, while appearing to differ (i.e., differing in emphasis), should logically be compatible.[13] Knowledge of certain aspects of the phenomenon is, to be sure, not a substitute for knowledge of other aspects. Nor is a part of a true conjunction, while true, the same thing as the whole conjunction.

In principle there is nothing illegitimate in *an* economic interpretation if it is not presented as an exclusive theory of human motivation and as an all-inclusive account of how and why changes occur. One is not obligated, in order to be objective, to present all possible knowledge of all the aspects in each treatment. No intrinsic error is involved in delimitation in the natural and social sciences.

The standard, then, is not completeness or certainty but factual grounding and compatibility with other known propositions. One can assume a higher degree of probability or reliability when assertions not only have empirical support but also accord with reliable theory in history and social science.[14] Or, as Walsh states it, the ultimate criterion of truth in history, as in all factual knowledge, is "the internal coherence of the beliefs we erect on that foundation." [15] This is implied by the logic of scientific method and has been exhibited historically in the process of cumulative analysis in various fields. It is also representative of current theories of knowledge. Fundamental coherence of established facts and theories is the test of objective scientific knowledge in any field. We have presented a theory of historical knowledge,

[12] Morton G. White, *Social Thought in America* (New York: Viking Press, 1949), pp. 226–228.

[13] *Ibid.*, p. 226; and see Hook, Bulletin 54, p. 126. Note that this compatibility is strictly on the level of factual theory, not on the level of value interpretations.

[14] See E. W. Strong, "Criteria of Explanation in History," *Journal of Philosophy*, 49:64–67 (January 31, 1952).

[15] W. H. Walsh, *An Introduction to Philosophy of History* (London: Hutchinson's University Library, 1951), p. 93; also pp. 76 f. See also Hook's statement, Bulletin 54, p. 126; and Arthur E. Murphy, *The Uses of Reason* (New York: Macmillan Company, 1943), p. 301.

but it does not provide any easy resolution of the problem of "the weight of the evidence," of conflicting testimony, of mixed motives, of influences on personality, of gaps in early records, or the overwhelming masses of modern documents.

Whether historians should make value judgments is a many-sided question. The fact is that they do. We cannot even discuss the "meaning of history" or, in common parlance, the "significance" of what has happened without introducing more or less explicitly some notions of value. Even the simplest terms in the historian's vocabulary carry value overtones: civilization, rise, fall, decadence, stability, progress, aggression, defense, cruelty, magnanimity. Without such value-words it would be very difficult to convey a sense of meaning, of the humane or the inhumane, the enlightened or the unenlightened. The aim of social science approaches in historical research is not only scientific knowledge—the how and the why—of historical processes, but also an understanding of their direction and meaning in relation to values. Social scientists do not avoid judgments and evaluations. They insist, however, that the bases for such judgments be explicitly stated, and that the "ought" of the historian be distinguished from the "is" of history.

The reactions to Bulletin 54, discussed in Chapter 1, indicated a growing awareness of the nature and function of value judgments. One commentator pointed to the fertility of conjectural hypotheses that were nonempirical; by such "unsupported theories" historians have discovered new facts and relationships. Moreover, he doubted whether a hypothesis applied with cold neutrality "could yield that full insight of which it is capable when it is the deep conviction of an original mind." [16] Another commentator concluded that the early zeal to make history "scientific" had enhanced "fact" and demeaned values and concepts. The problem, then, was to sharpen concepts and presuppositions, render them public, and facilitate rational discussion of conflicting hypotheses. Nor could values be ostracized. In so far as historians essay judgments on worth, they must publicly admit values to hypothetical status. [17]

The question may be put another way: what is the function of historians as transmitters of culture and what is their role in society? Something may be said objectively about the historical function of

[16] Willson H. Coates, "Relativism and the Use of Hypothesis in History," *Journal of Modern History*, 21:27 (March 1949).

[17] Bert James Loewenberg, "Some Problems Raised by Historical Relativism," *Journal of Modern History*, 21:17–23 (March 1949).

historians. Memory and literacy gave man "access to the past," and this capacity for transmitted learning became the basis for the function of history in the society and culture. Historians contributed a part of the memory of the past, and even helped to change or "revise" that memory or understanding. That memory in turn had influence on norms and values, whether or not historians deliberately read such values into their works. Deeper analysis of the historical function of history and historians is needed before an empirical theory can be offered.

Guarantee of validity of judgments is not entailed by historical statements that are philosophical or about worth. It is hardly surprising that Walsh's four classes of "disagreement among historians" are all moral categories.[18] Unless we get beyond our present "beginnings" of a science of human nature, Walsh implies, history will continue to be severely limited in its cumulative analysis of justice or meaning in the historical process. But with others we believe that values eventually may be given more empirical status.[19]

Since historians in fact do make judgments, critical standards are imperative. Loose speculation about meaning in history is open to criticism as wishful thinking or worse; but speculation per se is to be judged by the results achieved. An open society that respects objectivity does not welcome judgments or metaphysical assumptions that are stated with dogmatism; nor does a pluralist society take kindly to a unitary conception of history. Criteria for any extended judgment or conception of history should be explicit and subject to the logic of relevance and coherence. Historians seldom essay the grand role of philosophers of history nor are they professionally trained to assume it; but some training in value analysis, semantics, and elementary logic might well be a part of their equipment.

Historians make an objective contribution to knowledge when they empirically explain values and their functions in history. Where there has been general agreement on a value, notes Hook, "we can speak of objective or verifiable progress." His example is elimination of disease, considered as a good.[20] Health, safety, and satisfaction of hunger have been cited as common modern values. In the case of elimination

18 Walsh, op. cit., p. 100.
19 Ibid., pp. 69, 71, 118. See also White, Social Thought in America, Chapter 13; notes and references in Gottschalk, Understanding History, pp. 111 f., 244; and Waddington, op. cit., p. 34.
20 Bulletin 54, p. 117.

of disease, the historian might find its acceptance as a value related to the introduction of medical science. Science might be studied, as Waddington intimates, as a creator of new values.[21] New values are likely to appear and to be empirically defensible when a change in factual knowledge permits society to recognize an "evil" not as misfortune or fate, but as a social issue about which it is possible to do something through new knowledge and new organizational principles.

ANALYSIS OF CAUSATION

Hume's challenge to the empirical school, his conclusion that causal analysis discovered nothing more than that one thing followed another, has been reasserted by twentieth century skeptics. No historian, to be sure, knowingly or by implication would commit himself to the classical fallacy of *post hoc ergo propter hoc*. Yet causal imputations appear in every volume of written history, wherever origins of changes are "explained." Conditioning factors, precipitating events, and decisive choices are normally discussed. Some historians, however, aware of the perplexities of dealing with causation, seek to reject "cause" and "effect" as naive animistic language. One can, of course, avoid the pitfall of classical Greek logic by refusal to argue over a remote "first cause." One can also avoid the fallacy of assuming a "key" cause. One cannot, however, take refuge in explanations that seem, but only seem, to avoid causal imputation. The historical approach, observes Morris Cohen, involves "an avowed or tacit theory of social causation." [22] Distrust of theory leaves assumptions tacit. Predictions as to consequences of certain conditions are not explicitly formulated and critically examined.

While causality was once studied on the assumption that necessary sequences and basic similarities would be revealed,[23] R. M. MacIver more modestly emphasizes comparative study of significant differences in similar cases: "To find the difference—the more or less, and the variant traits of the more and the less—and to establish the comparability of the situations is often no small task, but it is the preliminary requirement." [24] A reformulation of Mill's method of dif-

[21] Waddington, *op. cit.*, pp. 34 ff.

[22] See Morris R. Cohen, *The Meaning of Human History* (La Salle, Ill.: Open Court Publishing Company, 1947); cf. p. 86, *supra*.

[23] Morris R. Cohen, "Method, Scientific," *Encyclopaedia of the Social Sciences*, Vol. 10, pp. 392 f.

[24] R. M. MacIver, *Social Causation*, p. 149. See Bulletin 54, pp. 39 f. on the nineteenth century search for "laws" of social evolution.

ference is, in his opinion, "the key method of the search for causes." [25]
Causes are "the various conjunctures of things in the process of creating
some difference that arrests our attention"; while *effects* are particular
differences "manifested by things in their various conjunctures." [26]
MacIver also points out that individuals and groups at critical stages
in history make a "dynamic assessment" of their situation; and that
such historic assessments are based on contemporary ideas of social
causation. Underlying the assessment are assumptions as to whether
given trends are reversible or irreversible and predictions as to
whether given social controls can have causal influence on the future.
On this level—that of the study of theories of causality as recurrent
historical phenomena and as factors affecting historic decisions (for
instance, Ricardo's economic theories and their influence on the re-
peal of the Corn Laws)—historians can and do make contributions,
using traditional documentary methods. On a more advanced level—
that of the formulation and testing of hypotheses regarding social
causation—historians like other social scientists must experiment with
methods appropriate for the special purpose.

A prolific source of historical controversy is the problem of assigning weights to factors that have causal influence. Historians still
generate heat in discussing the relative importance of different causes
of the Civil War. From cumulative research there is general agreement as to "greater" as distinguished from "lesser" causes, but not
agreement as to the most important causes. This may sometimes be
the "key" cause fallacy.[27] Perhaps use of techniques for quantifying
data could reinforce the judgments of historians as to lesser and greater
causes. In the absence of methods of assigning precise weights that will
not be purely arbitrary, emphasis on particular causes depends in part
on value hypotheses. These are highly significant in suggesting the
meaning of history, providing tentative evaluations of particular causes,
motives, and consequences. But they do not solve the empirical problem of precise weights and combinations of factors that produce specified results. Present historical practice can predict possible alternative
outcomes, but does not ordinarily yield knowledge of causes sufficient
to permit highly accurate predictions.

There are other approaches to causation. Mahan's theory of sea

[25] MacIver, *op. cit.*, p. 65.
[26] *Ibid.*, p. 382.
[27] For demolition of Marxian and other "key cause" ideas, see *ibid.*, pp. 113-120.

power [28] and Turner's theory of the frontier involved causal analysis in terms of long-range process. Both dealt also with concrete events, their causes and results, but their primary analysis was of the "influence" of sea power and of the "influence" of the frontier. Studies of the long-range influence of an economic revolution or of a great institution, of the two-party system, of a great man, of concentration of great wealth, all deal with problems of cause. One of the most helpful studies of method cogently treats cause, motive, and influence as an interrelated whole.[29]

Concern for the weights to be assigned to causes involves a mathematical approach, quite properly seeking useful knowledge; but there are also high-level contemplative approaches that can be particularly suggestive as to long-range tendencies. The particular conceptions of history developed by Marx, Spengler, or Toynbee are of course still controversial; but their effort to diagnose tendency certainly illustrates the potentials of causal analysis. Spengler, for example, was more successful in showing the configurations and the "essence" of a culture and its over-all tendency than in demonstrating his particular concept of causal inevitability or "destiny." [30] The contemplative approach at its best is perhaps illustrated by de Tocqueville's *Democracy in America,* a keen study of processes at work at a given stage, their convergent tendencies, their probable future directions of change. By cross-sectional analysis of process and structure and appraisal of the whole, causes can sometimes be seen in the large.

DELIMITATION

That delimitation is essential in inquiries that seek answers to specific questions is a commonplace to historians. Other social sciences, however, may suggest wider ranges of questions and therefore different methods of delimitation. Whatever the delimitation, it should be sharp, that is, directly relevant to the questions that are being asked. The concept of social process may suggest a very broad delimitation, or a very sharp one, for instance, study of how particular people be-

---

[28] Alfred T. Mahan, *The Influence of Sea Power upon History, 1660–1783* (Boston: Little, Brown, and Company, 1898).

[29] Louis Gottschalk, *Understanding History,* pp. 209–250. See also E. W. Strong, "Fact and Understanding in History," *Journal of Philosophy,* 44:617–625 (November 6, 1947); and "How Is Practice of History Tied to Theory?" *ibid.,* 46:637–644 (September 29, 1949).

[30] But see the arresting discussion of causality in *The Decline of the West,* Vol. 1, pp. 115–160.

came associated or dissociated—the process in terms of domination, submission, indoctrination, adaptation, conflict, intolerance, anti-radicalism, loyalties, or the like. Or a study of social process might be delimited by focusing on a specific social group, a specific kind of social interaction, or a complex of identifiable institutions. Other delimitations are appropriate in statistical analysis of changing standards of living or other social trends and economic fluctuations.[31]

The process of delimitation does not restrict, in an ultimate sense, the possibility of considering larger and more general explanations. Delimitation is necessary in rigorous scientific investigation; but the outcome is cumulative analysis which eventually can deal with larger interrelationships on the basis of knowledge established in earlier, sharply delimited studies.

CHRONOLOGICAL AND TOPICAL METHOD

Inseparable from methods of delimitation are the chronological or topical breakdowns appropriate for different types of investigation. A shift from the historian's normal time sequence may be involved in the application of social science methods. The bondage imposed on historians by a chronological sequence based on presidential administrations, national politics, and wars is discussed in Chapter 7. Some social science approaches focus on the major drives of the culture rather than on chronological groupings of public events, which are often only transitory reflections of more fundamental forces and long-range social conditioning. Basic institutions, such as the family, the church, and the school, often do not appear on the surface to be as centrally related to events as they really are. Family, kinship, class, caste, and other aspects of social structure; economic fluctuations and trends such as competition, monopoly, productivity, and income distribution; social maladjustment in modern urban centers or declining rural regions; psychological frustrations and responsive attitudes—such subjects cannot be adequately presented in the narrative appropriate in chronological political history. The data and theory required by many methods in the social sciences involve a synthesis with its own special topical and chronological organization. In general, cultural change cannot appropriately be treated in short-span chronology. The normal time sequence might even be shifted to investigate concepts of social process in a sequence spanning one thousand years.

[31] Very suggestive on these and other delimitations is MacIver, *Social Causation*, Chapter 5.

Focus on the chronology of public events may lead to an unsafe reliance on traditional documentary methods when pitfalls might be avoided by use of more appropriate social science methods. Following the chronology of public events, a historian might look for data to demonstrate the effects of the depression of the 1930's and innocently cite figures on the increase of suicides, viewing them as correlated with business failures or the volume of unemployment; but statistical analysis shows that the correlation was not as obvious as one might at first assume.[32] Narrative chronology of events may lead at any time to the type of documentary fallacy described by Lincoln Steffens, who created a "crime wave" by issuing press releases that grouped unrelated crimes together until they looked like a formidable list.[33]

QUANTITATIVE METHOD

Errors induced by traditional chronological and documentary method emphasize the value of quantitative methods as part of normal historical training. In general, historians have made little use of quantitative methods. The subject is technical, and appropriate courses might well be offered by graduate schools so that historians wishing to employ statistical methods which have yielded valuable results in allied fields could acquire the necessary training. In any case, before utilizing quantitative data from social science studies or government statistics, historians would be well advised to seek the guidance of experts in the particular field whose data are to be used and to consult elementary treatises that warn against methodological errors. A historian might, for example, learn how to use index numbers for comparisons of productivity, price levels, costs of living, and estimates of purchasing power. Even for early periods, historians can use quantitative data to fill gaps in present knowledge. Where price and wage data are fragmentary, for example, one can develop a crude measure of real wages by relating money wages to the price of wheat, thereby determining the wheat equivalents of changing wages. By simple computations using price and wage statistics for the last hundred years, changing real wages can be expressed in index numbers.

The economist consulted by the Committee suggested that historians could make a contribution by searching for figures on productivity.

[32] See Frederick E. Croxton and Dudley J. Cowden, *Applied General Statistics* (New York: Prentice-Hall, 1939), p. 769.

[33] *The Autobiography of Lincoln Steffens* (New York: Harcourt, Brace and Company, 1931), Part 2, Chapter 14.

Many statistical devices are used in sociology and psychology for discovering norms and regularities in interactive behavior, both of groups and individuals. Redfield, studying urbanization with sociological methods, was able to set up standards of correlation which may be suggestive of types of hypotheses that can be tested by quantitative study.[34] Statistical studies may correct loose generalizations as to political trends. Changing trends in American sectionalism might be brought out by plotting statistical curves of party votes, whose tendency to rise or decline throughout the country from one election to another would be shown.[35]

COMPARATIVE METHOD

"History," said Maitland, "is the art of comparison." The validity of generalizations is more evident, the more they fit similar classes of cases. *Generalization from a single instance is dangerous.* It is exceptional, applying only to that single case unless it is shown that it generally holds for a particular class of cases. Comparison thus is a method to develop theory about classes of historical phenomena. But merely to compare is not enough. *"Comparison, without contrast, does not amount to anything logically."* [36]

Comparative methods provide ways to test some hypotheses. Where several types of phenomena are discovered to coexist over a long period, comparison of their relationships at different points in time may reinforce hypotheses concerning a causal connection between them. If one phenomenon varies whenever an associated phenomenon varies in some particular manner, one can tentatively assume a causal connection. This is Mill's method of *concomitant variation.* Assumptions of a necessary connection, however, are not warrantable unless one has examined enough cases, including cases that, while comparable, offer contrasts. For example, if a historian tests the hypothesis that

[34] Robert Redfield, *The Folk Culture of Yucatan* (Chicago: University of Chicago Press, 1941); "The Folk Society," *American Journal of Sociology,* 52:293–308 (January 1947).

[35] See charts in E. E. Schattschneider, *Party Government,* pp. 113 ff. The relationship between the number of electoral votes of the winning candidate and his percentage of the popular vote over the last fifty years indicates a decline of sectionalism as a factor determining swings in presidential elections.

[36] John Dewey, *How We Think* (Boston: D. C. Heath and Company, 1910), p. 89, italics ours. See MacIver, *Social Causation,* pp. 65 ff., 149 ff. for combination of comparison (method of agreement) and contrast (method of difference) and for the importance of isolating single differences.

there is a necessary relation between modern capitalism and democracy, he at once identifies cases where history reveals no causal connection. Many hypotheses relate to differences in degree rather than to
absolute differences; comparative method helps to bring out the more
or less. Quantitative measurement of differences is possible in many
areas of social science, for example, in voting shifts, population shifts,
and changes in distribution of wealth or in standards of living.

Comparison, a familiar method in history, can yield new results by
wider use of social science concepts. Comparative studies of several
broad culture areas at a given period may sharpen differences between
cultures and identify unique aspects whose importance might not
otherwise be apparent. Or such studies may reveal broad common
denominators in separate culture areas and necessitate qualification
of untested assumptions as to the importance of supposed differences
between cultures. Anthropological methods may assist historians in the
treatment of particular culture patterns that constitute national variations within a broader culture area. "Culture's essence," observes
Kluckhohn, "is that there is a conventional, arbitrary selection of one
of a number of possible functional modes of action." [37]

Care is necessary, however, in comparisons of cultures. One can
speak of specific French culture patterns, but one should guard against
any tendency to beg the question by implying a coherent whole
culture unlike the German or others. In anthropological method,
comparison of French, German, and American culture is a study of
variations within the same culture area; so also is study of American
culture in the North and South before the Civil War. While abstractions can be made at any level, we must examine comparable things
at the same level. It is legitimate to speak of Western or Islamic
culture (whole cultures) or to speak of American or French culture
(subcultures with national variations). One may distinguish and compare regional variants, class variants, or professional variants, such as
the culture of American college professors.

BIOGRAPHICAL METHOD

As history has developed as a social science, its critical standards
have diminished the extravagances of character assassination, filial
piety, and the worship of demigods. A well-recognized danger is the
tendency to overstress the creative influence and individual achievements of leading figures. One should distinguish conspicuousness and

[37] Minutes of Committee conference with Clyde Kluckhohn.

posthumous reputation from influence.[38] One should note differences between what a man thought and intended and what his followers, or a later school, believed that he affirmed or intended.

The tendency to exaggerate the influence and achievements of "great men" is related to the tendency to neglect external social and cultural developments that represent more momentous influences and achievements than those of particular leaders. In ascribing influence, one is dealing with the problem of cause. One can bestow influence glibly; or one can do serious social science research on the problem. Even in biography there may be no man so dangerous as the man who has no theory.

Historians, working seriously, have been evolving a social science theory of biography. They do not regard social and cultural data as ingredients only for stage setting and dramatic plot. Actions in the plot do not march, scene by scene, to a prescribed destiny. Decisions by a leader do not necessarily make a great event inevitable or a great conflict irrepressible. The *historical* essence of a biographical study is not likely to be historic contributions made by one man. The history of a culture, or even a subculture, a nation, or a section, is not to be comprehended in terms of great men any more than in terms of great books; in fact, the less so, the more the great men, great books, and great actions are abstracted out from their social situation. But a biographer who culls judiciously from letters, speeches, and the like, selecting evidence in terms of *relevance* to important historical problems, makes contributions to *particularized knowledge of general phenomena*. But this is only to repeat what historians generally assume. What may be added by other social science approaches in biographical research?

Ideas and actions of historical figures are relevant to a great variety of social and cultural phenomena. Sociology of knowledge, social psychology, psychological concepts of personality and perception, real motives and socially approved motives, and other ways of analyzing the interaction of the individual and society advance our understanding of how man's ideas and behavior are made and altered and how a leader sees only limited options and makes his decision. The study of decision making is an important new area for social science research.

Biographical study of a leader should grapple with the theoretical problem of leadership. To have no theory of the phenomenon is to leave assumptions tacit, not subjected to formulation and testing. To

[38] See Louis Gottschalk, *Understanding History*, pp. 233 ff.

develop criteria of leadership is to contribute to cumulative analysis. One way to conceptualize leadership is by the development of a typology. Personality types that are particularly representative and effective for a given position or profession are being studied by psychologists. One needs a field theory of personality; "external" factors, not just childhood training, set norms and incentives and influence motivation and codes of conduct. Social role theory is also relevant, and a certain amount of exploratory work has already been done by historians.[39] Investigation of the extent to which group norms of various types dominate the thinking and behavior of particular leaders should be standard practice among biographers.

By study of personality traits, analysis of social roles, and such aspects of the sociology of knowledge as can be applied to particular individuals, historians may contribute to new explanations of leaders and leadership, of the dynamics of personality formation, and of the relation of the individual to the group. American "robber barons," restudied in this way, conceived neither by a devil theory nor by a romantic approach, appear something less than pillars of society, something more than inexplicable and unconscionable deviates. Socially approved motives of productivity and creative methods in business can be identified if they are present, as well as the influence upon ethics of various pressures of institutional expediency. By a field theory of personality and hypotheses as to social roles, one escapes the myopia of seeing history only through written testimony or too exclusively through the eyes of the person one studies. Convergent social science approaches, applied to biographical data, offer opportunity to revise or add to older biographical explanations.

GROUP RESEARCH

Utilization of convergent approaches of various social sciences is highly advantageous in the study of complex problems; but the use of such approaches may well call for research by a group rather than by an individual. Increasing knowledge of the complexity of relationships in society, and the consequent tendency of historians to multiply or enlarge the areas and types of relevant data produce an intellectual dilemma. By enlarging the area of interest, one reaches a point of diminishing returns, for one cannot be an expert on everything. The use of conceptual approaches in history and experimenta-

[39] See p. 168, *infra*, especially footnotes 23, 24; and Thomas C. Cochran, *Railroad Leaders.*

tion with methods derived from other fields might significantly be advanced under the direction of a group of experts, not all of them historians. Group research may serve as a partial check against individual autisms and especially against single explanations. The nature of social science compels resort to a wide variety of intellectual skills; advisory and collaborating groups of experts can ensure avoidance of methodological errors and testing of multiple hypotheses. Group research can be a very stimulating experience, despite the time consumed in discussion and the costs in money and individual frustrations. Historians who are interested in group projects might find it useful to consult the rapidly growing literature on group thinking and semantic problems in collaboration between experts.

But group research, even when adequately financed and intelligently organized, is not the answer to all problems. The history of science up to the present suggests, indeed, that the invention of new techniques and fertile hypotheses has not ordinarily come from the work of bureaucratic organizations. The best cross-disciplinary work is carried on, not within a group of specialists, but within the mind of the individual investigator. Progress in history as social science depends in any case less on particular institutional arrangements than on a general widening and deepening of the channels of communication between historians and other students of human behavior. Before one can agree or differ, it is necessary to understand.

CONCLUSION

It should be stressed once again that theory and practice in history as social science are still in an experimental, exploratory stage. The nonhistorical social sciences offer, to those willing to learn, a wide range of concepts, hypotheses, and theories, many of them firmly based on careful empirical research. But to the historian this represents not a collection of finished products ready for use but a source of raw material which demands the development of proper techniques of exploitation before it can be made to produce something useful and valuable. This presents a challenge to the historical profession. That historians stand to gain substantially by intelligent and eclectic borrowing from the other social sciences can hardly be doubted. But it is quite conceivable that the opportunity may be missed, and that a few unfortunate or clumsy attempts to write history in terms most meaningful to the other social sciences may produce a revulsion of feeling and a group consensus among historians that "the time is not yet ripe."

There is nothing inevitable or certain about the future development of history as science or as art. It is easy to find reasons for declining the challenge. The traditional ways of doing things often seem the safest. The early attempts to use a new approach are bound to be crude and unsophisticated, and those who venture into unexplored territory risk not only their time and energy but also their professional reputations.

Nevertheless, there are several grounds for believing, not only that the new approaches to history are already being proved feasible and rewarding, but also that the prospects for further advance, assuming the survival of our present cultural values, are relatively bright. The barriers between the disciplines have been found by experiment to be not so very formidable after all, and especially those between history, that most unspecialized of all specialties, and other social sciences. Interdisciplinary cooperation has been so widely proclaimed as desirable that a definite revulsion against too much crossing of the frontiers has become evident. There is no real substitute for historical research demonstrating by example, not by precept, how social science methods can be used. The cumulative refinement of techniques and interpretations implied by the term "science" cannot be achieved by good intentions; it can be achieved by patient and conscientious work.

7 THE SOCIAL SCIENCES AND THE PROBLEM OF HISTORICAL SYNTHESIS *

In the field of American history, selected as the one with which most readers of this report will be familiar, the past fifty years of rapid progress in the development of social science methods and hypotheses have had surprisingly little effect on historical interests, content, or forms of synthesis. This statement applies to American history either as taught in universities and colleges, as presented in textbooks, or as reflected in general literature. The main props of a synthetic structure, erected more or less unconsciously by such gifted pioneers as Channing, Hart, McMaster, and Turner, are still securely in place.

THE NARRATIVE SYNTHESIS

The synthesis in terms of great men and a sequence of important or unique events still appears in historical thinking. This leads to a narrative organization in which the nation's presidents and its wars play major parts in both substance and periodization. It is not so much that the matters with which the social scientist commonly deals are altogether unnoticed; it is rather that they are treated as incidental to a narrative of men and events. For example, how different from the historian's usual definition of his task is that of economic historian Alexander Gerschenkron: "Historical research consists essentially in application to empirical material of various sets of empirically derived hypothetical generalizations and in testing the closeness of the resulting fit, in the hope that in this way certain uniformities, certain typical situations, and certain typical relationships among individual factors in these situations can be ascertained." [1] Yet it seems probable that

* This discussion in a slightly different form appeared in an article "The 'Presidential Synthesis' in American History," by Thomas C. Cochran, in the *American Historical Review*, 53:748–759 (July 1948), and is reprinted here by permission of the Editor.

[1] Alexander Gerschenkron, "Economic Backwardness in Historical Perspective," in Bert F. Hoselitz, ed., *The Progress of Underdeveloped Areas* (Chicago: University of Chicago Press, 1952), pp. 3–4.

most social scientists would readily subscribe to the Gerschenkron definition.

Objections to the prevailing synthesis of American history might be lodged by thoughtful scholars of many different points of view. Judged by the complex of values and standards that may generically be referred to as humanistic, a synthesis built around great men and events falls short of the mark. It satisfies a follower of Toynbee, for example, but little better than it does a disciple of Kroeber.[2] But in this chapter we shall discuss only its inadequacy in dealing with the types of problems in modern society that most interest social scientists, or what may be termed from their point of view the historians' lack of a satisfactory method of analysis.

To members of the disciplines that have to study the problems of industrial society, the events or trends with which the historian has traditionally dealt often appear to be surface manifestations that are not of the highest importance; and the studies themselves seem to many social scientists correspondingly limited. These social scientists would like historians to give more attention to such topics as the causes and conditions of economic growth or stagnation; the effect on enterprise of community approbation, competition, monopoly, and regulation; the social adjustments demanded by growing urban centers, new types of employment, and changing levels of opportunity; the psychological frustrations developing from urban impersonality, badly selected social goals, and altered family relationships; the origins and persistence of social manners, attitudes, and beliefs; and the nature of political action, leadership, and motivation. The rapid rise of such group problems has characterized history-as-reality in the last century and a half but, needless to say, they are not the central features of existing historical syntheses. Moreover, study of general European history writing indicates that this weakness is not confined to the history of the United States.

LIMITATIONS OF THE NARRATIVE SYNTHESIS

How has this situation arisen? What has caused this relative lack of communication between history and the social sciences?

An obvious part of the answer lies in the fact that the writing of history is a time-honored and traditional occupation long antedating

2 See Arnold J. Toynbee, *A Study of History,* Vol. 1–6 abridged by D. C. Somervell (New York: Oxford University Press, 1947); and A. L. Kroeber, *Configurations of Culture Growth* (Berkeley: University of California Press, 1944).

the modern emphasis on empirical method in the social sciences or present-day problems or source materials. The historical record prior to 1800 here or abroad is relatively scanty. The historian has to use the materials he can find rather than those that might best answer his questions. To begin with, for many ages these materials are largely governmental, and the fact that the modern syntheses were developed in a period of growing nationalism led to a still greater preoccupation with political sources. Historians, accustomed to confining themselves to these old and easily available records for the earlier periods, failed to make use of the new types of material which became available in the later nineteenth century. The habits of the older historian, educated to a scarcity of records, were perpetuated amidst a later-day abundance. Statistical data, specialized periodicals, new types of correspondence, recorded interviews, and the records of many organizations, profit making or otherwise, were all relatively neglected, while the traditional sources were reinterpreted again and again.

This tendency has been noted or implied in various ways from the time of Buckle and Green in England and of the graduate seminars of the 1880's in America. Yet, in spite of an increasing recognition of the importance and complexity of the elements in modern society that are but faintly reflected in important events, no mature "social science" synthesis of American history has been produced to challenge the traditional formula.[3]

The explanation of such a striking intellectual anachronism is bound to be subtle and complex, for if the conventional structure rested on one or two easily recognized errors it could not have withstood the pressures of new generations of historians. A long list of causes must therefore be investigated, the absolute importance of any one of which is hard to evaluate, but all of which together seem largely responsible for the general failure of historians to think or write as social scientists.

[3] Guy Stanton Ford pointed out the need for such a synthesis many years ago in "Some Suggestions to American Historians," *American Historical Review*, 43:267–268 (January 1938). High school textbooks reflect a social scientific approach more than college, but have not attempted any radical resynthesis. Henry B. Parkes, *The American Experience* (New York: Alfred A. Knopf, 1947), while presenting an interpretation based on conflicting social ideologies, rather than the usual narrative, does not in general employ social science concepts or methods. Thomas C. Cochran and William Miller, *The Age of Enterprise* (New York: Macmillan Company, 1942) offers a general synthesis based on the social sciences, but puts specific emphasis on the role of business. See also Caroline F. Ware, ed., *The Cultural Approach to History* (New York: Columbia University Press, 1940), and Merle E. Curti and others, *An American History* (2 vols.; New York: Harper & Brothers, 1950–51).

The written record itself, particularly when buttressed with systematic documentation, exercises a tyranny that has been commented on frequently by students of the nature of language but often overlooked by scholars in other fields. The mere fact that a previous writer has organized his material and phraseology in a certain way creates a predisposition in its favor. The later writer can no longer respond quite freshly to the original data; he may agree with or object to what has been said, but in either case his orbit of thought is likely to center around the existing interpretation. A. M. Schlesinger, Jr. and Joseph Dorfman, for example, may argue about the interpretation of "Jacksonian Democracy," but they both accept the traditional concept as central to the synthesis of the period. Charles A. Beard introduced new economic factors, but employed them within what was essentially the existing political synthesis. With its great quantities of traditional literature, and its lack of accepted conceptual tools for new theoretical analysis, history probably suffers more than any other discipline from the tyranny of persuasive rhetoric.

In still another way, the inner compulsions of writing have ruled the historian. The traditional basis of history has been effective narrative. The "great" histories of the past such as Gibbon's *Decline and Fall,* Macaulay's *England,* or Motley's *Dutch Republic* have been exciting "stories." Furthermore, since historians like to have their books published and are not averse to sales, the popular dramatic frame of reference has been used whenever possible. This general approach is often valid when applied to the actions of a single individual, but neither narrative nor popular drama is usually suited to the analysis of mass phenomena. While drama will still be found in the conflict and resolution of forces or in group challenge and response, this is likely to be drama on a nonpopular abstract level. The historian has, of course, been aware of this dilemma but, faced with the choice of retaining a misleading emphasis on colorful individuals and exciting events or of giving up the narrative style, he has clung as long as possible to storytelling and treasured most those source materials that permitted narration.[4]

By taking the written record that was easiest to use and most stirring from a sentimental or romantic standpoint, that is, the record of the

[4] The time and money that have been spent on collecting and publishing even relatively unimportant letters of famous statesmen, compared with that expended in trying to learn something of the norms of the society in which they lived, strikingly indicate the popular trend.

federal government, the American historian prepared the way for one of the major misconceptions in American synthesis: the primary role of the central government in our historical development. While political scientists carefully pointed out that up to World War I, at least, most of the normal governmental contacts of the citizen were with his state, and historians dwelt on the importance of sectionalism and state rights and joined with business leaders in emphasizing the laissez-faire doctrines that for a large part of the nineteenth century circumscribed the role of the federal government, the same men, influenced perhaps by nineteenth century European training, persisted in writing a national history revolving around presidential administrations and passing controversies over constitutional law. In the early stages of the economic development of each region, government and politics were in truth of great importance; but government was that of the state, and politics revolved around such material questions as loans or subsidies to banking and transportation, practices of incorporation, the degree of government ownership thought desirable, and how to secure honest administration. In a later stage of economic growth the states led the way in regulating business and economic activity in the public interest. In neither stage, prior to 1900, was the federal government of major importance except for the initial disposal of public land, adjustment of the tariff, and widely separate changes in banking policy. The sporadic transference of ultimate power from state to federal government by decisions of the Supreme Court and acts of Congress from the 1880's on at first freed certain citizens from state controls without imposing effective federal ones. Not until the first decades of the twentieth century was the theoretical shift in power implemented by much effective federal action.

The realistic history of nineteenth and even early twentieth century politics, therefore, whether viewed from the standpoint of political parties or of the community, should be built around the states. This, of course, imposes an enormous burden on the historian. The situations in from 13 to 48 states cannot be adequately described in a unified narrative; to have meaning they need to be seen in an analytical structure. Furthermore, the older state histories are inadequate as a basis for such synthesis. Scholars must first produce new monographs on business and government in the states, and new cultural interpretations of state politics.[5] Indeed, at present, a general American history

5 For studies of government in relation to economic life in the pre-Civil War period, see Oscar and Mary F. Handlin, *Commonwealth: A Study of the Role of*

has to be more a series of suggestions of what ought to be known than a comprehensive synthesis.

A somewhat similar obstacle in the path of the historian who approaches the problem of systematic analysis and the building of some empirically based hypotheses is the extent to which our knowledge of the past depends on the writings of a small group of cultural leaders. He will tend to see events not only through the eyes of men of more than average vigor, property, education, and intelligence but also in the light of the metaphors of those who wrote the most enduring and readable prose. The circle of possible deception is completed when the statements of such abnormal citizens are read back as typical of their class, section, or society as a whole, and the resulting analysis is used to explain still other situations. The brilliant John Taylor of Carolina was not the typical Southern planter, Susan B. Anthony's problems were not those of the average woman, nor was Herbert Croly a good representative of many phases of the progressive movement.

A major reason for this reliance on leaders is that historical data on average people and everyday situations are hard to find. What was the typical rural community of 1840 from the statistical standpoint? What were normal ideas among its average citizens? Until there are answers to such questions, generalizations regarding the role of ideas in social change must rest on tenuous deductions.[6] Both quantitative and typifying studies are sadly lacking. Some of these data can be obtained through better use of published and manuscript census reports; others will have to be obtained by sampling methods, governed by proper statistical controls. The normal ideas of the average citizen in any time and place will have to be assembled from many indirect sources, such as the speeches of astute local politicians who, knowing what their constituents wanted to hear, mirrored public prejudices; the blurbs of discerning advertisers who sought in local papers to cater to public taste; and the letters of businessmen discussing public reactions that vitally concerned the future of their trade. Such

---

Government in the American Economy: Massachusetts, 1774–1861 (New York: New York University Press, 1947), and Louis Hartz, *Economic Policy and Democratic Thought: Pennsylvania, 1776–1860* (Cambridge: Harvard University Press, 1948).

6 See Theodore C. Blegen, *Grass Roots History* (Minneapolis: University of Minnesota Press, 1947).

materials are relatively hard to find and to use, but there are many indications of their widespread existence.[7]

Research using such sources immediately brings the scholar to a level of social relations deeper than that of conventional historic events, and exposes another major reason for the persistence of the narrative synthesis. As long as history consists of a series of important unique acts, thought to symbolize or cause change in society, a narrative account based on national happenings has a certain logic. But once the historian penetrates to the level of the social conditioning factors that produce persons capable of such acts and tries to find the probability of the occurrence of any type of event, the acts themselves become a surface manifestation of more fundamental forces. While events are an indispensable part of the data of history, and even chance events, granting there are such, may have strong repercussions on their environment, the use of social science approaches focuses attention on the aspects of the event that reveal the major dynamics of the culture, the uniformities rather than those features that appear to be most colorful or unique. The latter elements, by definition not being representative of the general culture pattern, will presumably have only a limited effect or significance. Southern secession, for example, had its roots in cultural factors underlying such events as the tariffs, the acts of abolitionists, or territorial laws that seemed to produce the friction. These events are chiefly useful as clues to the nature of the basic differences between the sections. Similarly the American people in the early 1930's, facing a new cultural situation, displayed qualities of resignation not easily explicable on the basis of either the traditional or immediate events of their past.

Historical change on this level of basic social conditioning is, to be sure, a difficult and—in the present stage of social science knowledge —a highly speculative study. Furthermore, the large quantities of material to be examined and the various types of special knowledge

[7] For use of such material see Merle E. Curti, *The Roots of American Loyalty* (New York: Columbia University Press, 1946); Lewis E. Atherton, *The Pioneer Merchant in Mid-America* (Columbia: University of Missouri Press, 1939), and *The Southern Country Store, 1800–1860* (Baton Rouge: Louisiana State University Press, 1949); Thomas D. Clark, *Pills, Petticoats and Plows: The Southern Country Store* (Indianapolis: Bobbs-Merrill Company, 1944); Thomas C. Cochran, *Railroad Leaders, 1845–1890;* and Everett Dick, *The Dixie Frontier: A Social History of the Southern Frontier from the First Transmontane Beginnings to the Civil War* (New York: Alfred A. Knopf, 1948).

required often make group, rather than individual, research essential. The generally individualistic work habits of the historian, therefore, suggest another reason for the lack of historical scholarship in this area. But the topography of this field has been charted sufficiently to allow even individual historians to make rewarding sorties into its intricate terrain.[8]

RESEARCH REQUIREMENTS FOR A SYNTHESIS IN TERMS OF A SCIENCE OF SOCIETY

In the space of a single chapter one can suggest only a few of the many types of research that will help build a synthesis in social science terms. As a beginning, it should be possible with patience and ingenuity to assemble the large number of career lines of different types of social leaders, essential for a picture of who succeeded in the society and how. Beside the pattern of how men succeeded in fact, there should be further study, based on qualitative sources such as private correspondence, of the alternative goals that influenced men's expectations.[9] How did their "level of expectations" from material or intellectual standpoints vary? What was the true "American dream"? Such considerations would lead not only to a higher level of generalization in social history but to possible scientific comparisons between American and other cultures.

A more difficult excursion into the field of basic historical factors is the tracing of the changing character of family relations, including both the relationships within the family circle and the aims and aspirations of the members of the family in their real and imaginary con-

---

[8] For a number of suggestive articles, see *Conflicts of Power in Modern Culture,* a symposium edited by Lyman Bryson, Louis Finkelstein, and R. M. MacIver (New York: Harper & Brothers, 1947). Abram Kardiner and others, *The Psychological Frontiers of Society* (New York: Columbia University Press, 1945), and Daniel Lerner, Harold D. Lasswell, and others, eds., *The Policy Sciences* are examples of the type of social-psychological and sociological literature that merits the attention of all historians.

[9] See Frank W. Taussig and C. S. Joslyn, *American Business Leaders: A Study in Social Origins and Social Stratification* (New York: Macmillan Company, 1932); Mabel Newcomer, "The Chief Executive of Large Business Corporations," *Explorations in Entrepreneurial History,* 5:1–33 (October 1952); Cochran, *Railroad Leaders, 1845–1890;* William Miller, "American Historians and the Business Elite," *Journal of Economic History,* 9:184–208 (May 1949), and "The Recruitment of the American Business Elite," *Quarterly Journal of Economics,* 64:242–253 (May 1950); Frances W. Gregory and Irene D. Neu, "The American Industrial Elite in the 1870's," in William Miller, ed., *Men in Business,* pp. 193–211.

tacts with the outside world. Whether one uses a striking term like Kardiner and Linton's "basic personality" [10] or some time-honored word like "background" to cover the effects of familial conditioning, few scholars will deny the fundamental importance of this factor in shaping the course of civilization.[11] But the investigation of the precise reaction to change is difficult, calling for psychological and sociological knowledge seldom possessed by the historian, and hence the family seldom appears as a factor on the level of historical events.[12]

An additional deterrent to historical analysis is that there are many "American families" at any given period. The variation in conditioning between the family of a back-country mountaineer and a rural professional man, or a city slum dweller and a Park Avenue millionaire, may easily be greater than the variation between the Maori family and the Maricopa.[13] As in recent studies in cultural anthropology, such as *Plainville, U.S.A.* or the "Yankee City Series," half a dozen different types of families based on income and occupational levels must be studied.[14] The upper-class groups offer data in the form of memoirs, letters, and contemporary comments; [15] the poorer groups, particularly before 1890, offer only a challenge to the investigator. But

[10] Kardiner and others, *op. cit.*, p. viii.

[11] See, for example, Talcott Parsons, "Certain Primary Sources and Patterns of Aggression in the Social Structure of the Western World," in Bryson, Finkelstein, and MacIver, eds., *op. cit.*, pp. 29–48.

[12] See John Sirjamaki, *The American Family in the Twentieth Century.* For the earlier period Arthur W. Calhoun, in *A Social History of the American Family from Colonial Times to the Present*, assembled a large mass of random material that has been rather uncritically drawn upon by historians. Sociologists studying the dynamics of the family have been more interested in the inner psychological tensions than in tracing historically the changing external pressures that altered the patterns. See, for example, Willard Waller, *The Family: A Dynamic Interpretation* (rev. by Reuben Hill; New York: Dryden Press, 1951).

[13] The Maricopa are Southern Arizona Indians; the Maori are Polynesians. See also Clyde and Florence R. Kluckhohn, "American Culture," in Bryson, Finkelstein, and MacIver, eds., *op. cit.*, pp. 106–128.

[14] James West (pseud.), *Plainville, U.S.A.* (New York: Columbia University Press, 1950); W. Lloyd Warner and others, *The Social Life of a Modern Community, The Status System of a Modern Community, The Social Systems of American Ethnic Groups,* and *The Social System of the Modern Factory*, Yankee City Series, Vols. 1–4 (New Haven: Yale University Press, 1941–47).

[15] The biographer or historian has used these materials chiefly to enrich and support narrative, but to the cultural anthropologist or psychologist they present clues to social and psychological patterns. Social scientists have made as little use of these historical materials as historians have of the techniques necessary to analyze them.

the scholar striving to check theories and hypotheses regarding the family against historical data (and no one not so motivated should essay the task) will doubtless find many clues that have been concealed from the eyes of the conventional historian. Perhaps some day it will be possible to guess wisely at the degree to which group aggressions, political radicalism, or instability in mass reactions were due to the stresses and strains of a family conditioning that became unsuited in varying degrees to the changes in surrounding society.

Looking at the situation more broadly, the new social-psychological problems of Western civilization by 1900 can be seen as the result of contrary types of conditioning: in youth, family and school conditioning, based either here or abroad on mores and folkways largely inherited from a pre-industrial society; in maturity, conditioning in urban offices and factories, based on new mores and folkways that were evolving from the needs of business; and almost from birth to death, conditioning by pulpit, press, or other media of communication, based on a heterogeneous mixture of traditional and pragmatic doctrines.[16]

Shifting attention on this fundamental level to the rise of urban industrialism, the chief external pressure that upset existing family patterns, one enters a field where historians have done considerably more work but have in general subordinated their findings to the events of the narrative synthesis, and have failed, because of their disinterest in theory, to deal with many of the problems basic to urban sociology. Even A. M. Schlesinger, Sr. who did much to start study of urbanism by historians and whose general synthesis in the latter half of *Land of the Free* is one of the best, keeps the city in a relatively subordinate position.[17] Special areas of sociology of first importance, such as urban demography and its social consequences, are not properly considered in our general histories.[18] The whole argument might be summed up by saying that we have many "social" accounts of American historical data but few sociological interpretations.

In all this confusing historic picture of shifting ideas, folkways, and mores, of new family relationships and of growing urban problems,

[16] See Thurman Arnold, *The Folklore of Capitalism* (New Haven: Yale University Press, 1937); and Elton Mayo, *The Human Problems of an Industrial Civilization* (New York: Macmillan Company, 1933).

[17] Homer C. Hockett and Arthur M. Schlesinger, *Land of the Free* (New York: Macmillan Company, 1944).

[18] See, for example, Sidney Goldstein, "Patterns of Internal Migration: Norristown, Pennsylvania, 1910–1950," Ph.D. thesis, University of Pennsylvania, 1953, dittographed.

the massive physical force producing change has been industrialism. Yet, judging from the narrative synthesis, the obvious fact that it was industrialism that moved us from the world of George Washington to that of the present day apparently needs still more emphasis. The spearhead of the multiple pressures of industrialization has been business, and businessmen have been of necessity the human agents who transmitted to society most of the physical changes born of science and industrial technology. The institutions of business, therefore, became the central mechanisms in shaping a new society and imposing industrial customs upon it. Before mid-century, the sensitive New England intellectuals were well aware of the change. Emerson complained in 1844:

In America, out-of-doors all seems a market; . . . I speak of those organs which can be presumed to speak a popular sense. They recommend conventional virtues, whatever will earn and preserve property; always the capitalist; the college, the church, the hospital, the theatre, the hotel, the road, the ship of the capitalist,—whatever goes to secure, adorn, enlarge these is good; what jeopardizes any of these is damnable.[19]

From 1840 to 1860 the new impact of business and its urbanism upon American culture was perhaps greater relatively than in any other equal period, yet such forces appear only in the form of a few isolated phenomena in the usual treatment of the pre-Civil War era.

In the post-Civil War years the continuing cultural pressures of business, on which the War itself had relatively little effect, are better recognized by general historians. But a new difficulty now appears. Just as in the case of public opinion, the family, or urbanism, the spectacular and exotic rather than the normal have tended to find their way into the traditional synthesis. Our textbooks, for example, tell much of the resistance of certain farm groups to elevator and railroad practices but little of the growing force of business folkways and mores in the rural community.[20]

In this case the approach to a more comprehensive and meaningful

[19] Ralph W. Emerson, "The Young American," in *Nature Addresses and Lectures and Letters and Social Aims* (Boston: Houghton Mifflin Company, 1921), p. 388.

[20] See, again, West, *op. cit.;* and also the extensive bibliography of older sociological studies of the rural community in Walter A. Terpenning, *Village and Open-Country Neighborhoods* (New York: Century Co., 1931). More recent analyses, such as Paul H. Landis, *Rural Life in Process* (New York: McGraw-Hill Book Company, 1940), are still weak in tracing the gradual infiltration of business mores and folkways in the rural community.

synthesis will be much easier than in those previously discussed. Business records of all types are becoming available in increasing quantities.[21] Monographic reports are steadily accumulating.[22] The general historian surveying this field, however, will find that while existing studies in economics and in history give much of the internal picture of the workings of business, the connections between business and society are not elaborated.[23] The business leader or entrepreneur, for example, was the arbiter not only of change within his company but also, to a large extent, of change in his community.[24] Since his money, and hence his approbation, was generally necessary for community welfare and improvement, he sat on the boards of the educational, charitable, political, and business institutions that dominated social customs and set social goals.[25] And necessarily, he carried into these other fields the patterns of behavior formed by the needs of survival in business. He strove to make education, charity, politics, and social life "businesslike." Generations of historians have analyzed the thought of Clay, Webster, and Calhoun to extract every last vestige of social meaning, while Nathan Appleton, John Murray Forbes, and a host of other important business figures of the same period, awaiting their

[21] A National Records Management Council has been organized and is preserving business records and training business archivists.

[22] See the *Harvard Studies in Business History*, Vol. 1–16 (Cambridge: Harvard University Press, 1931–50); and the New York University Graduate School of Business Administration, Business History Series, Vol. 1–2 (New York, 1948).

[23] See such studies of the current situation as Robert A. Gordon, *Business Leadership in the Large Corporation* (Washington: Brookings Institution, 1945); and Peter F. Drucker, *Concept of the Corporation* (New York: John Day Company, 1946). N. S. B. Gras, *Business and Capitalism* (New York: F. S. Crofts and Company, 1939) is a historical study of business organization. Some studies, such as Carl F. Taeusch, *Professional and Business Ethics* (New York: Henry Holt and Company, 1926), and Max Radin, *Manners and Morals of Business* (Indianapolis: Bobbs-Merrill Company, 1939), deal with limited aspects of the relations of business to society. Cochran, *Railroad Leaders, 1845–1890,* Chapter 15, deals with social ideas and social role.

[24] See Arthur H. Cole, "An Approach to the Study of Entrepreneurship," *Journal of Economic History,* 6(suppl.):1–15 (1946), for general discussion of the socio-economic role of the business leader; Thomas C. Cochran, "The Social History of the Corporation in the United States," in Ware, ed., *The Cultural Approach to History,* pp. 168–181, for discussion and bibliography on social aspects of business; and William Miller, ed., *Men in Business.*

[25] See, for example, Hubert P. Beck, *Men Who Control Our Universities* (New York: Kings Crown Press, 1947), and Merle E. Curti, *The Social Ideas of American Educators* (New York: Charles Scribner's Sons, 1935), pp. 210–232.

first full-length social interpreter, do not appear in the traditional narrative.[26]

The modern corporation, a new social instrumentality developed primarily by business leaders, must also be given a much larger place in this more meaningful synthesis. Here the problem is a very difficult one, challenging the scholar not so much from the standpoint of data or materials for research as from that of theory. The role of the corporation in modern society has never been adequately analyzed by legal, social, or economic theorists. Noncorporeal, but quite real, the corporation of both the profit and nonprofit variety has established substates and subcommunities within our political and geographical divisions.[27] It has created both highly responsible and highly irresponsible entities with which all citizens are forced to deal, and under the influence of which most citizens spend a large part of their lives. Ownership as represented by stock in large corporations has become a functional relationship. Control of the property has passed into the hands of professional, and frequently nonowning, administrators.[28] The resultant problems of historical interpretation are too complex to discuss here, and have been in fact too complex for the wisdom of modern society, but complexity and difficulty are not valid excuses for historical neglect.

In summary, at the center of any comprehensive and meaningful synthesis, determining its topical and chronological divisions, should be the material and psychological changes that have most affected, or threatened most to affect, such human conditioning factors as family life, physical living conditions, choice of occupations, sources of prestige, and fundamental beliefs. While the historical analysis itself, in the present stage of psychological knowledge, must be concerned with concrete physical, political, or social changes or events, these should be assigned place and importance on the basis of their estimated relation to underlying social forces. The precise social effects

[26] For Appleton, see Frances W. Gregory, "Nathan Appleton, Yankee Merchant: 1779–1861," unpublished Ph.D. thesis, Radcliffe College, 1949.

[27] For discussion of the subcommunity or subgovernmental aspects of corporations, see A. M. Schlesinger, "Biography of a Nation of Joiners," *American Historical Review*, 50:1–25 (October 1944); and Stuart A. Daggett, *Chapters on the History of the Southern Pacific* (New York: Ronald Press Company, 1922). For some suggestions concerning needed studies, see Charles A. Beard, "Corporations and Natural Rights," *Virginia Quarterly Review*, 12:335–353 (July 1936).

[28] See Oswald W. Knauth, *Managerial Enterprise: Its Growth and Methods of Operation* (New York: W. W. Norton & Co., 1948).

of the rapid rise of the corporation from 1850 to 1873, for example, have not been examined, but the social scientist is reasonably sure that they are of more importance than the details of presidential campaigns.

For the period since the middle of the nineteenth century, there is available source material for an amplified synthesis based on changes in major social forces. While present knowledge leads us to believe that business and economic changes should be recognized as the most dynamic elements in this particular place and period, further investigation may reveal alterations in family life or in social beliefs not stemming directly from business sources as more powerfully operative. But as long as the historian will equip himself with the knowledge necessary to probe these deeper levels, and approach the problems in the spirit of scientific analysis, social scientists will applaud the results as steps in the direction of historical realism.

Such a backbone of synthesis would not only place the narrative structure of events in proper perspective but would alter the look of most of the other familiar landmarks as well. War studied as a social institution would preserve its importance, but war as an arbitrary milestone for historical periodization would probably disappear. The Civil War, for example, that great divide of American historiography, shrinks in magnitude when viewed in the light of these long-run social criteria. Even in the deep South, the dramatic change in race and property relations brought on by the war will lose some of its importance when measured against the full background of the gradual social changes coming from the increase in middle-class farmers and industrial workers.[29] In any case, for nations as a whole, basic social change seems to come less cataclysmically than is indicated by wars or revolutions. Periodization should be recognized as wholly arbitrary and dependent on the central focus of the synthesis employed. From the business and economic standpoints, for example, 1850 and 1885 are available points for periodization, the one symbolically marking the beginning of the rapid opening of a national industrial market, the latter roughly coinciding with the rise of a number of large semimonopolistic business units and the beginning of federal regulation; but if the family or urbanism is made the central phenomenon other dates might be selected.

For those historians who will mourn the passing of the historio-

[29] See, for example, Herbert Weaver, *Mississippi Farmers, 1850–1860* (Nashville: Vanderbilt University Press, 1945).

graphic sway of Jeffersonian and Jacksonian Democracy, the Era of Good Feeling, the Irrepressible Conflict, the Tragic Era, the Square Deal, the New Freedom, and the New Deal, there is the poor consolation that time must doom the ancient subdivisions. When the United States is even two hundred years old instead of a hundred and seventy, it will no longer be possible to discuss all the traditional men and events. Broader and less detailed syntheses will be demanded by the exigencies of space and time, and it will be up to the historian to choose whether he will attempt an intuitive resynthesis of the type presented by Spengler or Toynbee, or avail himself of the aid offered by the social sciences.

INDEX OF NAMES

INDEX OF SUBJECTS